Advance Praise

"*Be Different: Listen Purposefully. Love Courageously. Live Intentionally* is a devotional that will tempt you to read ahead! Leah's personal stories, clear biblical translations, and inspiration will tease you to keep reading. But don't! Her call to deep reflection will ignite the change and transformation in you that you most need right now. Her words are a bridge between our earthly reality and spiritual growth. This is a meaningful, timeless, and profound must-read!"

—**BRENDA K. REYNOLDS**, TEDx speaker, coach, and author of *TBD—To Be Determined* and *5 FROGS Transformation Journal*

"*Be Different* masterfully bridges the gap between biblical teachings and the contemporary challenges women face today in a way that feels both profound and accessible. Each chapter unfolds with grace, reminding readers that living differently is not a burden but a journey to true freedom and joy."

—**MICHELLE HILL**, pastor, speaker, and founder of Women Connecting in Prayer

"A gentle, shame-free guide to cultivating extraordinary, healthy interpersonal relationships based on biblical principles. This insightful devotional is a must-read for anyone seeking to love in a way that can truly change the world."

—**KELLY D. HOLDER, PHD**, clinical psychologist

"There is a time to be silent and a time to speak. *Be Different* invites you to do both. Through biblical teachings, prayer, and answering provocative questions, a new voice will emerge in a new person. It's a transformative experience."

—**ANN MICHAEL DORGAN**, CEO, QUALIA Intangible Asset Management

"All I can say is wow! Leah's book *Be Different: Listen Purposefully. Love Courageously. Live Intentionally* truly ministered to me. This devotional is for anyone who is looking to grow spiritually while facing life's challenges. Leah's candid and down-to-earth approach in sharing her personal journey makes her highly relatable. This book not only offers insights for self-reflection but also guides you in making the essential changes needed to align with your true calling from God."

—**PATRINA O'CONNOR-PAYNTER**, nonprofit executive, media personality, and speaker

"Leah's *Be Different* beautifully blends practical wisdom with deep spiritual truths. This inspiring must-read empowers you to embrace change and live with more love and intention."

—**CAMILLE TROTT**, CEO of Austin Communications, leadership consultant, and executive coach

*To Dear Suwada,
Love, Melissa*

A DEVOTIONAL EXPERIENCE

BE DIFFERENT

LISTEN PURPOSEFULLY.
LOVE COURAGEOUSLY.
LIVE INTENTIONALLY.

LEAH JM DEAN

HOUNDSTOOTH
PRESS

Copyright © 2025 Leah JM Dean
All rights reserved. No part of this book may be reproduced in any form without prior written permission from the author and/or publisher.

BE DIFFERENT
Listen Purposefully. Love Courageously. Live Intentionally.

FIRST EDITION

ISBN 978-1-5445-4724-4 Hardcover
     978-1-5445-4723-7 Paperback
     978-1-5445-4725-1 Ebook

Cover Design: Pixie Grotto Studio, Bermuda
Cover Photo: Brenton Alexander @brentonalexanderphoto

The personal stories in this book are based on the experiences of the author and have been constructed for illustrative purposes only. Unless specifically requested, all the names of the individuals in this book have been changed. Where individuals are identifiable, they have granted permission to the author and the publisher to use their stories and/or facts about their lives.

To every woman and girl who believes
"God's not finished with me yet!"

CONTENTS

Hello, Lovely. Welcome! 1

PILLAR ONE
LISTEN DIFFERENT 8
   1. I Need You to Listen 9
   2. Lessons in the Silence 15
   3. The Download 23
   4. The Formula 27

PILLAR TWO
TRUST DIFFERENT 38
   5. The Power to Stay 39
   6. Foolish or Unfoolish Hands 45
   7. The Quest for Significance 49
   8. It Was Never What We Were Told Anyway 55
   9. Remember the Lion and the Bear 61
   10. Why Me, Why Now? 67
   11. Stuck in a Cycle 73
   12. Good Enough 79
   13. Raise the Bar 83

PILLAR THREE
THINK DIFFERENT 92
14. The Ultimatums 93
15. The God Gift 97
16. A Messy Tribe 103
17. If You Don't Know Me by Now 107
18. Whatever It Takes! 113
19. Not Today 117
20. What Are You Treasuring? 121
21. The Stories We Tell Ourselves 125
22. Captive Thoughts 129

PILLAR FOUR
TALK DIFFERENT 136
23. But Why Did You Need to Search? 137
24. The Power in the Pause 143
25. Avoid Avoiding Conflict 147
26. Fruit-Laced Parables 153
27. Speak Softly and Carry a Beagle 157
28. Don't Sink My Boat 161
29. Heal the Scab 167
30. A Voice That Changes the Atmosphere 171

PILLAR FIVE
LIVE DIFFERENT 180
31. Out with the Old and on with the New? 181
32. A Blessing with a Boundary 187

33. When Friends Betray You 193
34. One Moment at a Time 199
35. Moments of Margin 205
36. A Praying Tribe 211
37. Loving Different While Living Different 215
38. Love Anyway 221
39. With All Your Heart 225
40. Salt 229

Final Thoughts: The Chameleon Effect 237
Acknowledgments 243
A Special Invitation 247
About the Author 249
Bringing Be Different to Life 251
A Special Request 253
More Books by Leah JM Dean 255
Bible Translations 257
Endnotes 259

HELLO, LOVELY.
Welcome!

I'm so glad you're here! I'm sure if I could sit down with you right now, you'd have lots of stories. Stories of how you've loved people and how at other times they've been the source of your deepest pain. But no matter how fast and how far you want to run, you need people, and they need you. We know this because almost every human who has ever walked the face of the earth at some point has wanted it—that urge to talk and just be heard, the gentle touch of a friend, the wet kiss from a child, the helping hand from a colleague, or a smile from a stranger.

So, we put in the work. We let down our walls and search for our tribe. We pour our time, energy, and heart into building trust and nurturing our relationships. In those moments when we feel truly loved and supported, we believe relationships are worth the effort. But then, there are the tougher times—when the rubber meets the road, and we find ourselves in need. Sometimes, despite all we've given, we face rejection or silence and it still feels like we're facing life all alone.

God knows. Think about it. From the beginning of time, God knew loving and living with people would be a roller coaster. Imagine the pain of choosing to sacrifice your son so you could save your other children. If that wasn't hard enough, imagine having to watch as your child was hatefully and gruesomely killed.

Despite all of the pain people can bring, God still wants everyone in this divided, crazy world to feel His love. However, His plan is different—by human standards, risky even. He decided to use relationships to shape destiny. His plan involves using the hands of people like you and me. In God's word, His Son Jesus reminded us, *"A new command I give you: Love one another. As I have loved you, so you must love one another. By this everyone will know that you are my disciples, if you love one another." (John 13:34–35 NIV)*

The simple truth to transforming how you live and experience relationships is to understand that you are called to **Be Different**. All your life, when it comes to people, you've been aching for the simple when God has commissioned you for the complicated. You've been waiting for the "people coaster" to stop when God is calling you to feel it, experience it, and impact lives through it.

When I think about all of the amazing stories of how God has used the hands of people to touch the lives of characters in the Bible, my life, and the lives of others, I've come to understand that being different is not a status we achieve. It's deeper. It's a way of life. A daily, challenging, beautiful, painful, yet exciting, sometimes momentary journey rooted in five foundational pillars.

I think of pillars as principles or values that influence how we show up every day. Here's a summary of the five Be Different pillars so you can get a clearer picture of what I mean:

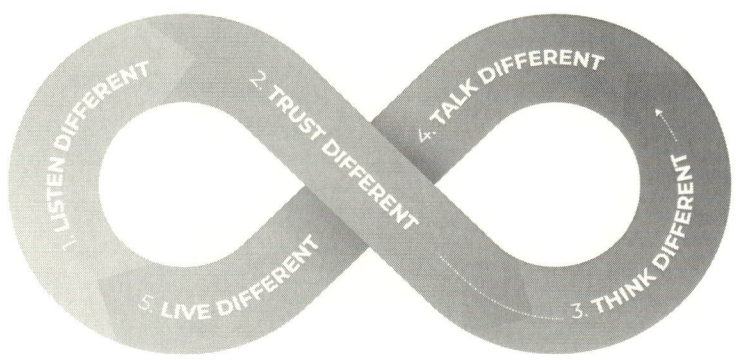

Pillar One—Listen Different: What might happen if I blocked out the noise of life so I could clearly hear God's voice?

Pillar Two—Trust Different: Can I believe that no matter what life sends my way, God will supply everything I need? Can I trust and accept that I'm enough, God's perfect custom design?

Pillar Three—Think Different: In what ways do I need to challenge my relationship expectations of others?

Pillar Four—Talk Different: How can I be more intentional about using my words to be clear but kind and speak life into people and situations?

Pillar Five—Live Different: What would it look like to show up every day and act in ways that demonstrate God's love, no matter how I feel?

What You Can Expect from *Be Different*

This devotional experience includes forty bite-sized chapters that you can read in seven minutes or less. The chapters are broken into sections based on the five Be Different pillars. At the beginning of each section, I'll share a brief introduction to the pillar. Then, each chapter starts with a question and a scripture, offering a gentle foundation for the reading. At the very end of each section, I'll recap all of the questions to give you an opportunity to reflect on what God has shown you and where He may be calling you to grow.

So how should you read this book? I only have one rule: There are no rules! Read it in one sitting or enjoy making this your daily devotional for the next forty days or so. Underline, highlight, write in the margins, or grab your favorite journal to capture your thoughts as you go. Read it by yourself, or read it with a group so you can talk and support each other by sharing experiences. My hope is that you'll think of *Be Different* as a trusted companion you can come back to again and again.

If you're anything like me, as you read, you may find you're stuck or struggling with one of the pillars. As you turn each page of this book, please know that's okay. I believe you didn't just pick up this book because of the cover art or something someone said. You picked up this book because, for you, this is a divine appointment. God wants you to experience lifelong transformation in your heart and relationships so that through your touch, people will experience His love.

Now stop and imagine that a good friend drops by your house, puts their arm around your shoulder, and says, "Girl, you know what? I think there's a better way to do life with people."

My hope for you is that reading the pages of *Be Different* will feel like that warm conversation. Full of stories and God moments that'll help you shift from drained, bruised, or buried to healed and restored.

I've prayed for you, and I'm excited for you. I hope you're ready to see what God's going to do.

Let's get started!

XO,

Leah

listen
DIFFERENT

PILLAR ONE

Listen Different

Welcome to Pillar One of this devotional experience. In these next few chapters I share my story. As you read, reflect on your own journey.

In what areas of your life are you seeking clarity from God?

In a world filled with noise and busyness, there's so much peace and power in learning to be still.

God is always speaking. The question is, are you listening?

1

I NEED YOU TO LISTEN

IS IT TIME TO PAUSE AND LISTEN FOR GOD'S DIRECTION IN YOUR BUSY LIFE?

*"My sheep listen to my voice;
I know them, and they follow me."*
—John 10:27 NIV

I was the global head of human resources, and a fellow executive had stopped by to ask for my help. I don't recall what we were talking about. Maybe it was a deal, an employee issue, or possibly recruitment for a new role. Whatever it was, by the time we wrapped up, he had exactly what he needed and was bubbling over with praise.

Out of the corner of my eye, I could see the sun glistening through the window as I watched him walk across the room. The door closed, and as I heard the latch quietly click shut, an overwhelming feeling of shame settled over me like a heavy, suffocating blanket. As I paused to reflect on his words, out of nowhere a quiet little voice assaulted me. "Leah, the woman he sees at this moment is not the same woman who shows up at home and with her tribe. And she's *definitely* not the same woman who walks through the doors of her church every weekend."

You see, I was tired.

Every day I started at zero and ran until I pushed myself past one hundred.

My motto was: "Excellence is not a singular act, you are what you continually do" (attributed to Aristotle).

Every day I was doing the most, trying to be everything to everybody, and I was exhausted.

On top of that, my belief in God also required a commitment that trumped my feelings on any given day. *"Whatever you do, work at it with all your heart, as working for the Lord, not for human masters." (Colossians 3:23 NIV).* You see, in the end, God was my real boss.

Even though most days I loved the challenge, that didn't make it easy. You see, where there are people, there are complications. And for me, the daily churn of the corporate engine and the world of HR, with all its policies and practices, sometimes felt like a ship hitting the rocks of the reality of people's lives.

On a personal level, it was a struggle as well. Every morning, I was up at five to work out and start my day, but still, my weight bounced up and down like a seesaw ridden by two aggressive five-year-olds. If all of that wasn't enough, something unexplainable was happening as well. Even though I had no clue what was going on at the time, what I now know as perimenopause showed up early and uninvited at my doorstep. In spite of all of that, at work most days I was able to show up with confidence. But on some occasions, as one of the few female leaders in the company, I still felt the "onlyness"—the feeling of loneliness you get when you're the only one in the room —set in.

On the home front, it was no different. Two young kids, homework, one on one time, birthday parties, cooking, all while trying to be a good wife. In some ways, my family—in particular, my husband —has always been my counterbalance. To this day, I can still hear my husband's voice in my head: "Just relax, we don't need gourmet meals and lots of company. Cheerios will do just fine."

In fact, during one conversation with my then eleven-year-old son about my value of excellence, he looked at me and said, "But Mom, does everything really have to be excellent?" In the moment, I was stumped into silence as I wondered if my values had become too tall a measuring stick for my life.

After all the work and home life, then came my tribes. There were so many relationships where I simply didn't have time. As a person who enjoys close connections, I struggled with drive-by meetings and shallow hellos. I needed time with my people!

My solution: Organize regular get-togethers at the house. I would spend hours cooking and preparing the house for guests, only to pass out on the couch from exhaustion while my guests were still there!

At church, the story repeated itself. I loved my roles and ministries. I was passionate, opinionated, and always looking for ways to improve things and help us operate "more effectively." With my high standards and overflow of ideas, I struggled with anything that was unorganized or "last minute" or anything that got in the way of our careful planning. I often became frustrated, and even when I didn't voice my frustrations, resentment was building on the inside. What had once been a weekend oasis of praise and worship was twisted into what felt like a weekend prison of tasks, duties, and long meetings.

As a result, I became a woman who walked through the doors at church no longer excited and wanting to serve. I was tired. Actually, I was exhausted. And even though I tried to be patient and loving, more often than not I found myself missing the mark. At some point, I shifted from loving and serving to just getting it done. It was just another series of tasks that needed to be completed with complicated people, and frankly I was tired. And, by the way, I'm not putting myself on a pedestal here; I believe every human being is complicated, including myself.

Perhaps you can relate to some parts of my story, or maybe even to all of it. You're trying to give everyone and everything your best, but somewhere along the way, life starts to get overwhelming and you lose your sense of peace.

I believe the woman who pursues peace and love will place herself on a path to build the kingdom of God. When we ask God to help us show up differently in our relationships, we give Him free rein to provide the people, predicaments, and problems to reposition us to become His hands on earth and to share His love.

However, that day in my office, as I turned to look out the window, peace and love were the furthest things from my mind. It was as if I was staring into a mirror and a stranger was looking back at me. Lost in this sudden train of thought, I felt the weight of my life and complicated relationships on my shoulders. I also felt…shame. As I rolled this unexpected barrage of thoughts over and over again in my mind, I heard a still, small voice say to me, "Leah, it's okay. I'm not here to crush you with shame. But it's time to make a shift, and I need you to listen."

As I stood up to leave my office for the day, I had no idea what God was doing or the process He would take me through so I could fully understand what that shift would mean. Little did I know He was setting me up to hear Him more clearly and experience relationships in a whole new way.

As we close out this first devotional reading, let's pause for a moment to pray. In fact, at the end of each chapter I'll invite you into a moment of prayer. These moments will be your opportunity to ask God to help you Be Different. To lend you His strength to be His hands on earth and become the woman He's calling you to be. Let's pray.

Prayer

Dear Father,

For so long, one of my deepest prayers has been to hear Your voice. To understand Your purpose for my life—how You would use me, and the lives I would impact. For too long, I have allowed the pressures of life and my desires to bury the gentle prodding of Your Spirit. God, in this moment, I pray we can start over. I want to hear from You. I want to be Your hands. As I take this journey with You, please reveal Yourself to me like never before. I'm ready!

Amen.

2

LESSONS IN THE SILENCE

HOW CAN YOU BE MORE INTENTIONAL ABOUT FINDING OR CREATING SPACE TO PAUSE?

"...my immediate response was not to consult any human being. I did not go up to Jerusalem to see those who were apostles before I was, but I went into Arabia. Later I returned to Damascus. Then, after three years, I went up to Jerusalem..."
—Galatians 1:16–18 NIV

Something had to change. Didn't the voice say I needed to listen? Something had to give. So, when the opportunity came to step down from my volunteer positions at the end of the year, I made a mad dash to resign and get off at the very first exit.

Initially, I enjoyed the peace of walking away, but something felt amiss. You see, growing up with parents who've actively served in church and the community for more years than I've been alive, I was still wired to get involved. So, as was my custom, I prayed and asked, "God, what do You want me to do?" In the past, the answer had always been clear.

"Move here, take on this responsibility, or shift in this direction."

However, this year was different. As I prayed and prayed, there was nothing but…silence.

Initially I didn't resist. No weekend or evening meetings. It all came to a grinding halt. With so much still on my plate, it was easy to stay away. Yet, the tug to serve persisted, prompting me to pray. But each time, my plea was met with no answer, just deafening silence.

Initially, family, friends, or church members would ask, "How are you? When are you coming back?" After a while, they stopped inquiring. Or someone would say, "We were just talking about you when we went through our 'missing members' list." In those moments, I felt judged, and it became easier to stay away.

Months went by, and I kept asking, but still, there was silence. Over time my prayer shifted from "God, what do you want me to do?" to "God, if it's me getting in the way, change me so you can use me."

Over the years, I've wondered why God kept me in that silent place. It wasn't until I wrote this book that God finally revealed why.

Sometimes, God takes us to a silent place to teach us things we can't hear when we're so busy.

Let's take another look at the Bible passage for this reading. In the first chapter of Galatians, it's clear that Paul didn't consult with anyone when God called him to ministry. Have you ever experienced what it feels like to finally be clear about your mission, even if it's just for a season? I know when I've felt it, I want to dive right in.

While a natural reaction might have been for Paul to share this experience with others or seek guidance from early church leaders, he chose a different path. Led by the Spirit, he entered a season of silence to fully receive the details of God's assignment for his life before stepping into his role of preaching and teaching the early church. You can read the full story of how Paul was called to ministry in Galatians 1:11–24.

As I thought about Paul's story, it became clear that when God wants to reveal His plan for our lives, sometimes He needs us to be quiet. In that moment, God had me look back over the years since that day in my office, and I immediately saw everything He had been teaching me. From my silent place, He'd taught me how to hear His voice, how to delve deeper into His word, how to forgive, how to take leaps of faith, how to trust Him, and how to build tribes that change the world. As I sat there, I was blown away by what God was doing and teaching me, all from my silent place.

I thought I was done. Then suddenly, I felt an urge to pick up my pencil. I began to write down seven signs that it might be time to spend some quality quiet time with God.

Sign 1—We Stop Growing

When we stop carving time out of our busy schedules to spend time with God, like any relationship, our connection stagnates and stops growing. Just imagine what might happen if we never spent time with our parents, spouse, or child. I'm sure that would lead to a lot of distance, pain, or even dysfunction. God wants more for our relationship with Him.

Sign 2—We Stop Bearing Fruit

The fruit of the Spirit is love, joy, peace, patience, kindness, goodness, faithfulness, gentleness, and self-control. I don't know about you, but I've found on my own strength, living these qualities consistently is impossible. We can't be loving, peaceful, or anything else on our own. Staying connected to the Spirit allows us to access the fruit we need daily in our relationships.

Sign 3—We're Exhausted

Perhaps on more days than we'd like to count, we're tired, grumpy, and plain old done. When we wear ourselves out doing all the things and run ourselves ragged, this is a sign we might need to be silent so God can help us set our priorities.

Sign 4—We Can't Hear God's Voice

Often, when we're in this exhausted place, we can't distinguish between the voices in our head and God's voice. He's always there, willing to speak. However, if He can't get a word through, this could be a sign that we need to be still.

Sign 5—We Struggle to Forgive

If we find ourselves struggling to let go of past hurts and pain, this could be a sign that it's time to get in the silence. God needs to heal our brokenness. You see, forgiveness was never for them; it's for us. God wants to set us free.

Sign 6—We Stop Building Tribes

Perhaps we're hurt, and we can't trust people. Or maybe we've found the perfect church family or small group, and we feel like we're finally home. So, we isolate ourselves. God said to me, "This is a sign." Our greatest mission in life is to share God's love with others. We can't accomplish His mission if we always choose to stay comfortable with our community or close ourselves off from the possibility of new relationships.

Sign 7—We Forget Who and Whose We Are

We might just need to enter into silence if we're trying to do life on our own. Day after day, we might be grinding, trying to work in excellence on our jobs, with our families, or in our communities. We're trying to make it happen. God said to me, "I'm not governed by any rules. I can send you to a quiet place or elevate you in any space." When we're exhausting ourselves trying to help God out, it might be a sign that it's time to be still.

As I digested each sign, I realized God had pushed me to a place of silence that day in my office. All those years of asking God, "What do you want me to do?" and not getting a response was because I was exhausting myself, focusing on all the wrong things, and God had a *lot* of work to do inside me.

God's coming back for people who know Him, hear Him, and represent His character—and whom He can use. I hope you know and can feel it. God has a plan for you, too. Ephesians 2:10 reminds us that, like Paul, you are a masterpiece. Before you were born, God had a purpose for your life. He custom-designed a mission for you, lives you would impact, and change you would bring about. But sometimes, you might need to be still so you can hear His voice. Because sometimes, the best lessons, the clearest instruction, and the most profound clarity about God's plans for your life—and the people you're meant to touch—aren't found in doing, but in simply being with God. And sometimes, just sometimes, the path to being is discovered in the silence.

Prayer

Dear Father,

It's a new day, and I'm so thankful. I'm grateful for the reminder that clarity about Your purpose, mission, and best next steps for my life can be found when I spend time with You! In a busy world with so many pressures and a society literally designed to steal my attention, could You help me prioritize You? Thank You for these seven reminders of just how much I need to be still. God, I recommit to spending time with You and ask You to help me make You the number one priority in my life.

Amen.

3

THE DOWNLOAD

**HAVE YOU ASKED GOD
TO HELP YOU LIVE OUT HIS
PLAN FOR YOUR LIFE?
IF NOT, WHY?**

*"Call to me and I will answer you,
and will tell you great and hidden things
that you have not known."*
—Jeremiah 33:3 ESV

I spent at least a year and a half, maybe even two, in that silent place. Over and over, I prayed, "God, what do You want me to do?" and still, there was no answer. After some time, I began to feel guilty; shouldn't I be doing more?

I now look back and clearly see my heart was not ready to return to ministry or community service. However, at the time, I was anxious to "do" something, so I kept asking, "What do You want me to do?"

One bright and beautiful Sunday morning, I sat at my kitchen table, looking out the window, drinking a cup of tea. In the quiet of the moment, I asked again, "God, I really do want to know; what do You want me to do?"

And just as clearly as if I was talking to a friend on the phone, I heard God say, "Leah, I want you to use everything you have learned and experienced to help women and girls."

God couldn't have been clearer. The next year, with the help of my tribe, I held my first women's event. The event was three days with thirty-seven women and twelve girls. The mood was electric as people networked, discovered their strengths, and learned new personal and professional skills. We were so excited. We planned a second event two months later, asking every attendee from the first event to bring a friend. It was a New Year's wellness event with sixty-six women in the room. We had a blast.

That night the team came over for an after-party. We had a great time laughing and relaxing, and they left sometime after 1:00 a.m. I fell asleep blissful and content. Only, a good night's rest never came. Just a few hours later, at 5:00 a.m., I woke up with a start.

In the still of the morning I heard the Spirit's still, small voice say, "Go to your computer."

A little dazed, I thought, *It's a little early. I don't want to get up*, as I turned to fall back asleep.

However, sleep wouldn't come. "Go to your computer!"

But I just fell asleep and I need more rest. Yesterday was a long day! I thought to myself.

"Go to your computer!"

Slightly disoriented, I stumbled out of bed and sat down at my computer. Then the ideas started to flow. In less than an hour, I had the outline for my first book, *Assemble the Tribe*. I knew I was onto something, so I decided to commit to waking up every Sunday morning to write. Then the book started to form. The book was about helping women embrace their unique value, find belonging, and build thriving communities.

As the book began to take shape, I started sharing some of the ideas and concepts with a few close friends. One day, one of them asked me to speak to the women at her church. I was about a third of the way through writing the book, and so I thought, *What a great opportunity to see what the Bible has to say about finding and building female tribes"*

I began to research female tribes of the Bible, which frankly was a little depressing. The relationships often involved backstabbing and complications—for example, Leah and Rachel, Sarah and Hagar, Mary and Martha. Nothing but heartbreak and drama. I decided to switch tactics and look at male tribes: Daniel and his friends, Job and his friends, to name a couple. Try as I might, each of these stories still lacked the guidance I was looking for about relationships, so I continued searching. Then I began to read the story of Christ, and that's when everything changed!

After reading and rereading the story of Christ, I typed these simple words onto my PowerPoint slide: I have value. I belong and so I love.

The concept was still a little raw; however, as I put the finishing touches on the presentation, I knew this was just the beginning. I was listening and couldn't wait to understand more deeply what God had to say.

I believe that, just like He spoke to me, God wants to speak to you, too. Maybe it's time to get into the silence and listen. All He wants is you.

Prayer

Dear Heavenly Father,

Thank you for reminding me that You want to spend time with me. You speak through sermons, books, people, and Your Word. However, I'm reminded You also want to speak directly to me. God, I humbly ask You to show me Your plan for my life. Tell me where to go, where to walk, what to do, and what to say. I give You my heart and my life all over again. I'm open and I'm Yours.

Amen.

4

THE FORMULA

WHAT TRIBES DO YOU HAVE OR NEED TO BUILD?

"And your ears shall hear a word behind you, saying, 'This is the way, walk in it,' when you turn to the right or when you turn to the left."

—Isaiah 30:21 ESV

After more than a year of reflection and study, the words *I have value, I belong and so I love* evolved into a simple formula we can use to create community: Believe + Belong = Be Different®.

BELIEVE
If we believe in our value as human beings

+

BELONG
and have found any place to belong

=

BE DIFFERENT
we can leverage our belief and belonging to be OPEN to new relationships and THRIVE in the relationships we have

Let's explore how this formula can transform our relationships and our lives.

Believe in Your Value

Before the world was even formed, there was a plan. This plan was gut-wrenching and heartbreaking. It would entail separation, brokenness, rejection, disappointment, and betrayal. Sound familiar?

When Jesus walked the earth, He knew who He was and whose He was. He was aware of His purpose and the plan. He was to be both the Savior and the sacrifice. As difficult as it was, only two choices remained: death or a lost humanity…forever.

Imagine yourself in His shoes for a moment. From the time He was old enough to fully understand His calling, every single hour of His life was a step closer to a planned and prophesied harsh and brutal end. Each day that He lived, He had to remind Himself that His mission was greater than His misery and that every moment of His days on earth would impact your eternal destiny. So, what did He do? He spent His time tending to the needs of the poor, sick, and disenfranchised, teaching them how to live and love.

In the Sermon on the Mount, recorded in Matthew 5, He reminded us that no matter our background or standing in society, even if we're the lowest of the low, God wants to bless us. Often, we're searching for purpose when God is asking us to believe that we have value. That just by being who we are and sharing our gifts with others, we're living out our life's assignment.

Find Belonging

As I began to digest that, like Christ, we all have a God-given purpose, I started to wonder, what role did people play in His mission? When Christ was ready to start His ministry, the first thing He did was fast and pray for forty days. Shortly thereafter, He assembled His tribe: the disciples.

I think that's a *big* deal! Jesus was fully God and fully man, and one of the first things He did after fasting and praying was find a group of men to support Him and His mission. I believe this is a reminder for us when we want to live out our purpose: a great place to start is with silence, prayer, and fasting. But it's important not to miss that Jesus also demonstrated that when our calling is transformational, it will never be accomplished alone. We all need a tribe.

So, what is a tribe, you might ask? In my first book, *Assemble the Tribe*, I share my exploration into the history and meaning of the word. Long story short, I define a tribe as individually complex people who choose to come together in various ways to create relationships. Let's consider this in the context of Jesus' ministry.

If I were Jesus, on the most important mission in the history of the world, I would have some very specific criteria for my tribe. But when we look at the disciples, they were a complicated bunch. In selecting them, Jesus demonstrated that all kinds of people can add value to our lives.

In addition, He demonstrated that sometimes when interacting with our tribes, we might connect with some people more deeply than others. From His disciples, He called the twelve, and from the twelve, He had an inner circle of Peter, James, and John. In doing so, Jesus modeled that we'll experience different levels of intimacy with different people, and that's okay.

Not only did Jesus have different levels of intimacy, but He also had different tribes. You see, I've always thought a tribe was a close group of people I could do life with and that's all I really needed to survive. But Jesus had a different approach. While our instincts might be to find one group and stay there, Jesus did something else. Day in and day out, He ministered with the disciples, but He had other relationships as well. There were Mary, Martha, and Lazarus and the women who supported his ministry. He also spent time with friends, dignitaries, and even strangers He met during his travels.

I think this is important because sometimes, at different stages in your life, you might think you have enough community. You have your friend circle or small group at church, and you probably feel you don't need anyone else. Jesus demonstrated that we need multiple tribes and when we stay open to connecting with new people, they can support us in accomplishing our mission or be there for us in times of great need.

Be Different

This last part of the formula is where things really started to change for me. During His ministry, Jesus beautifully demonstrated what it means to Be Different. He assembled and poured into His disciples. They walked together, talked together, ate together, and learned together. He even taught them about self-care when He pulled them aside to rest. However, they didn't just connect with each other and stop; they supported Jesus as He taught, healed the sick, and raised the dead. In doing so, they demonstrated what kingdom living looks like, our call to Be Different.

The lesson for us: Build tribes for safety and support, but don't just get comfortable and stay put. Our tribes are springboards into purpose and becoming God's hands on earth.

One of the things I love about God is that He often starts us in a place we recognize while He's preparing us for more. You see, I never spoke to my friend's women's group. To this day, the presentation is still filed away on the desktop of my computer. I thought I was writing a book about how to build female tribes when all the time, God really wanted me to understand that everything I believed about relationships needed a total makeover.

Since releasing my first book, I've spoken to thousands of women across the world who want to unlock the formula for building tribes and experience life-changing relationships. However, more often than not, I hear their pain:

"Why am I struggling to believe that I'm enough?"
"Why have my tribes hurt and rejected me?"
"How do I survive the pain my relationships bring?"
"Why is it so hard to _____ (fill in your relationship challenge)?"

As you contemplate these questions, my prayer for you is that you find a renewed passion for making time and space to listen to God's voice. It could be the Spirit's still, small voice; something you read or watched; wise words from a friend or spiritual mentor; or a series of life-altering events. No matter the form, God is always wanting, always yearning to speak to you. The text in this reading reminds us that not only does God want to speak, He is prepared to be specific. The question is, are you ready and willing to listen?

Pillar One is complete. I hope in my story, you've seen how God can speak to a worn-out, messed-up person trying to do "all the things" on her own strength. If He did that for me, I promise He wants to do the same for you, too.

Prayer

> Heavenly Father,
>
> Thank You so much for leading me to this place. In Your Son's story, I can clearly see I need people. My prayer is that I'll never be without You, and I'll find my tribe(s) and live out Your purpose for my life. God, some days I'm so busy doing I don't know how to stop and get into a quiet place so I can listen to Your plans. Please slow me down, teach me, show me, and change me. I humble myself to listen to Your voice in a whole new way. I'm open. I'm Yours.
>
> Amen.

UNLOCK MORE: If you feel called to deepen your understanding of building strong community, I invite you to explore these additional resources. If you want to delve deeper into the formula for building and thriving with your tribe, visit leahjmdean.com/bedifferenttribe. Take your time with the quiz, and let it be a moment of self-discovery. Reflect on how you define "tribe" and the overall health of your community. After that, if you're ready to take the next step, visit leahjmdean.com/bedifferenttribe and embark on the DARE journey to start building your tribe with intention and purpose. Remember, you're not alone. My hope is that these tools will strengthen and support you every step of the way.

Reflect & Renew

Finding the time and space to pause and ask God about His plans for our lives can often be a challenge. As we wrap up this first pillar—Listen Different—take a few moments to reflect on the questions we have explored in our journey so far. Ask God to show you where He wants you to grow.

LISTEN DIFFERENT

1. Is it time to pause and listen for God's direction in your busy life?
2. How can you be more intentional about finding or creating space to pause?
3. Have you asked God to help you live out His plan for your life? If not, why?
4. What tribes do you have or need to build?

trust
DIFFERENT

PILLAR TWO

Trust Different

You are enough.
Just be who you are.

O n the surface, the idea of being who you are seems like the exact opposite of trying to be different. However, how often does your inner critic or self-doubt creep in? Telling you you're not enough? I believe that's all about to change.

Proverbs 23:7 says what we believe about ourselves shapes who we are. In the next few chapters, we'll start right where the enemy begins—your mind.

Welcome to Pillar Two: Trust Different.

Imagine a life with less doubt and more confidence and joy.

Embracing who God created you to be, even when it feels uncomfortable.

5

THE POWER TO STAY

IN WHAT WAYS CAN YOU LEAN ON GOD TO HELP YOU FIGHT AND WIN YOUR BATTLES?

"'Get out of here, Satan,' Jesus told him. 'For the Scriptures say, You must worship the Lord your God and serve only him.'"
—Matthew 4:10 NLT

To set the stage as we kick off this pillar—Trust Different—let's go back to just before Jesus was about to start His ministry. During His baptism, the heavens opened, the Spirit of God descended like a dove, and a voice from heaven spoke: "...This is my Son, whom I love; with Him I am well pleased." (Matthew 3:17 NIV)

We turn the page to Matthew Chapter 4 and find that Jesus was led into the desert by the Spirit to be tempted by the devil. Isn't that just how life is sometimes? You're connecting with God, and before you can even blink, temptation or a battle for your mind is right on your doorstep. Jesus had been fasting for forty days and nights. It was when He was in this tired, worn state that the enemy made his move. But God was making a move too. Jesus' encounters with the devil are a powerful master class on how to strategically fight off the enemy's attacks. Let's dig in.

Strategy 1—Stay Connected

During their first encounter, the devil said to Jesus, *"'…If you are the Son of God, tell these stones to become loaves of bread.' But Jesus told him, 'No! The Scriptures say, "People do not live by bread alone, but by every word that comes from the mouth of God."'" (Matthew 4:3–4 NLT)*

It's no coincidence that the first thing Satan tempted Jesus with was food. Have you ever faced a food *if*?

"If I eat the cookie, I'll feel better."

"If I could just get my hands on some buttery, soft, warm bread…"

"If I could curl up on the couch with a bag of chips or a pint of ice cream, I could erase the misery of this day."

Both science and scripture (read Daniel 1) make it clear: Food plays a huge role in our physical and mental well-being. From personal experience, I've seen how even small changes in my diet—positive or negative—can dramatically impact my life.

But here's the truth: Just like he tempted Jesus, the enemy will tempt you, but temptation does not have to end in failure. Instead of letting the enemy's *ifs* throw you off course, let them remind you how important your mission is. Wars and battles are won by making strategic moves, with support—and you are not alone. Stay connected to God's strength to help you overcome even the most tempting *ifs*.

Strategy 2—Stay Armed

The enemy will attack when you're preparing for your assignment or when you're at your weakest. When you feel tired, worn, hungry, or exhausted, this is the perfect opportunity for the enemy to attack your mind. In these moments remember, God hasn't changed His plans for you. This is simply the test in your testimony. Like Jesus, stay armed with scripture so you can use the weapon of God's word to fight the enemy.

Strategy 3—Stay Focused

Then the devil took Jesus to Jerusalem, to the highest point of the temple, and said, *"...If you are the Son of God, jump off..."* Jesus responded right back and said, *"The Scriptures also say, You must not test the Lord your God." (Matthew 4:6–7 NLT)*

Did you notice that over the course of these first two encounters the devil says to Jesus, *"If you are the Son of God"* twice? One of the enemy's greatest tools is to make us doubt who we are. Your doubting *ifs* might sound like this:

"Can I really take that role?"

"Will God protect me if I make this move?"

"Who am I to write a book, lead a Bible study, or [place your assignment here]?"

In your weak moments, stay focused on who and whose you are. You are God's child (John 1:12), fearfully and wonderfully made (Psalms 139:14), and covered (Psalms 91:4). Stay focused.

Strategy 4—Stay Vocal

In their final encounter, the devil tried a different kind of *if*. He took Jesus to the peak of a very high mountain, showed Him all the kingdoms of the world and their glory, and said, *"I will give it all to you…if you will kneel down and worship me." "'Get out of here, Satan,' Jesus told him. 'For the Scriptures say, "You must worship the Lord your God and serve only him."' Then the devil went away, and angels came and took care of Jesus." (Matthew 4:9–11 NLT)*

When the enemy gets in your face and tempts you with *ifs*, get vocal just like Jesus did—talk back! We can tell the enemy where to go and we can claim the many promises in God's word, like this one:

> *No, in **all these things** we are more than conquerors through him who loved us. For I am convinced that neither death nor life, neither angels nor demons, neither the present nor the future, nor any powers, neither height nor depth, nor anything else in all creation, will be able to separate us from the love of God that is in Christ Jesus our Lord. (Romans 8:37–38 NIV)*

You have weapons. Stay vocal. Talk back!

Strategy 5—Stay Alert

At the end of this final exchange, Matthew reports that the devil went away, and the angels came and took care of Jesus. It's a beautiful thought that we have the comfort of the Holy Spirit and our angels in times of need. However, that's not the point I want to leave with you. When Luke recounted that moment, he gave us a little more insight: *"When the devil had finished tempting Jesus, he left him until the next opportunity came." (Luke 4:13 NLT)* This reminds us, our battles with the enemy are not a one and done. He's going to come back again and again with his temptations and *ifs*. Stay alert.

I used to wonder why the Spirit led Jesus into the wilderness to be tempted. On the surface we might see the wilderness as a place of isolation and struggle. But time and time again in the Gospels we see Jesus head off by Himself into the wilderness to connect with God and be filled with the Holy Spirit.

Jesus' wilderness experience reminds each of us that we can trust God and the power of His word in all circumstances. When we seek God through prayer, fasting, and His word, He equips us with everything we need for the battles we face. I don't know about you, but I'm so thankful we have the wilderness and the word as powerful weapons to fight off the enemy's attacks and give us the strength to stay.

Prayer

Dear Heavenly Father,

    I'm thankful. I'm grateful that when I'm attacked again and again, I can push back on the enemy. The enemy can't do anything for me or give me anything that You cannot supply. Father, when he tempts me or speaks doubt into my life, remind me that You're there and help me to trust You. Please speak to me and show me in Your word how to drown out his voice and stay grounded and anchored in You. Lord, I know it's just a matter of time before I face this battle again. I'm encouraged because, like You were with Jesus, You will be with me, too. Thank you.

    Amen.

6

FOOLISH OR UNFOOLISH HANDS

HOW MIGHT ADOPTING THE WAY GOD
SEES YOU IMPACT YOUR LIFE?

*"A wise woman builds her home,
but a foolish woman tears it down
with her own hands."*
—Proverbs 14:1 NLT

A few years ago, a friend invited me to join her on a forty-day fast. It was the first time I'd ever fasted for that long. I stripped my diet down to fruits, vegetables, nuts, and gluten-free grains. The transformation was amazing. The pounds melted away, my mind was firing on all cylinders, and my heart connected with God on a deeper level.

Then, the fast came to an end. The timing coincided with some kind of celebration, and now I could eat! I was still praying and worshiping, but the focus on fasting from food to focus on God began to shift. Little by little, I tore down the forty days of healthy habits. A few months later, I found myself the heaviest I'd been since giving birth to my children.

Has there ever been a time in your life that mirrors my experience? You invest countless hours in self-work to understand and believe in your value. You pray, worship, attend conferences and workshops, or read books. You learn about your gifts, talents, and strengths, and then, bit by bit, you build up your physical, mental, emotional, professional, or spiritual muscles and begin to share them with others.

Then it happens. That event, person, or moment triggers an old or new trauma or awakens insecurity. Perhaps a loved one or friend told you they no longer wanted a relationship. Maybe it was a boss who reminded you day after day that your work was not good enough. Or maybe it was a spouse who crushed or ignored your dreams. When that trauma or trigger occurs, something in your mind translates it all into: I'm not good enough.

With that significant, sometimes subtle, and even unconscious trigger, the cycle of tearing down begins. Tearing could mean running to food when the stress increases. That delicious cake or pasta becomes your safe place, your moment of release. Tearing down could also be the mental and emotional self-beating that occurs every time you say or do "that thing." In your struggle to push through, your belief in your value vanishes, and you begin to wonder, *Do I even matter?*

There will always be people who don't like or value your gifts. I can also guarantee life is going to hand you circumstances that may cause you to want to self-destruct. The beautiful thing is that God has promised He will always be there. He always wants, yearns for, looks for, and values you. I love how David, the psalmist, confidently speaks about his worth to God: *"I praise you because I am fearfully and wonderfully made; your works are wonderful, I know that full well."* *(Psalms 139:14 NIV)*

The same David who had many failures as a father. The same David who committed adultery. The same David who orchestrated *murder*. Yes, that same David. Even in his imperfection, he praised God confidently, believing he was valuable. The same God who made David controls the winds, waves, sun, moon, stars, oceans, and flowers. The same God who also sets up kingdoms and tears them down made you precisely the way you are and values you so much that He sent His Son to die on a cross just for you!

"A wise woman builds her home, but a foolish woman tears it down with her own hands." (Proverbs 14:1 NLT) Your opportunity in this moment is to reflect on who God says you are:

- ∞ *You* are known—Isaiah 49:15–16
- ∞ *You* are God's child—John 1:12
- ∞ *You* are chosen—1 Peter 2:9
- ∞ *You* are wanted—Isaiah 43:1

God created you, loves you, and has so many beautiful plans for you. Ask Him to help you end the cycle of building up and tearing down once and for all. He's there waiting, loving, and wanting. It's your time, wise woman. Start now.

Prayer

Dear God,

I need Your help. I've experienced so many things that often lead me to, without even realizing it, tear down who You created me to be. Lord, reset my mind, replace my words, and help me to get off the roller coaster of building up and tearing down. Help me to share all the gifts You have given me with others just like You planned. Thank you for a fresh start.

Amen.

7

THE QUEST FOR SIGNIFICANCE

WHAT STEPS COULD YOU TAKE
TO BELIEVE IN YOUR VALUE
EVEN WHEN YOU'RE NOT DOING
SOMETHING BIG?

*"But the Lord said to Samuel,
'Don't judge by his appearance or height,
for I have rejected him. The Lord doesn't
see things the way you see them.
People judge by outward appearance,
but the Lord looks at the heart.'"*
—1 Samuel 16:7 NLT

According to the Merriam-Webster dictionary, significance is the quality of being important, having notable worth or influence.[1] If you're reading this book, I'm sure you want to live a life of significance, doing what God has called you to do. However, you're human, and from time to time, the yearning for a life of significance can sometimes become intertwined with the question, "Am I significant?"

One day, as I was out for my early morning walk, I was confronted with this very question. You see, I had left the corporate world and what I believed were positions of significance. As I walked the streets and looked into the offices on every side, I started comparing what I used to do with what I was building, and a feeling of insignificance began to creep in. While I was pondering these unsettling thoughts, the story of Haman in the Book of Esther came to mind.

In the story, Haman was one of the most "significant" men in the entire kingdom. The Bible states, *"…King Xerxes promoted Haman son of Hammedatha the Agagite over all the other nobles, making him the most powerful official in the empire." (Esther 3:1 NLT)*

Even though Haman was second only to the king, he had a significance issue. People bowed down to him everywhere he went, except for one man: Mordecai. Haman was consumed with rage when he experienced this lack of respect. Upon learning of Mordecai's nationality, Haman decided it wasn't enough to harm Mordecai. Instead, he looked for a way to destroy all the Jews throughout the entire empire. (Esther 3:5–6)

You may know the story well, but if you don't, I encourage you to read the entire Book of Esther. Here's a quick recap: Haman's plan leads the queen to risk her life by exposing his plots to the king. In the end, Esther's petition and Haman's actions result in his execution on the very gallows he had built for Mordecai.

So what can we learn from Haman's story? Haman sat in a seat of significance above all others. In that seat, he had power, influence, and authority exceeding everyone other than the king. In that seat, Haman could command change and bend situations to his will. Imagine all he might have accomplished in that seat! But his need for significance was ultimately his undoing.

In my reflections on the story and character of Haman, it struck me that there are a few ways significance may cause us to struggle:

Struggle 1—Fight for Significance

Maybe you're like Haman. You've been promoted to a seat of significance at work, church, or in your community, but some people refuse to respect your role and authority. No matter what you do, they resist and disrespect you at what appears to be every turn. That lack of respect can leave you angry, hurt, and frustrated. These feelings make it easy to become distracted. Instead of focusing on all the lives you can impact and the change you can influence, you get stuck fighting the politics or mess of your emotions, and your opportunity for impact is lost or marginalized.

Struggle 2—Desire for Significance

Maybe you struggle with feeling insignificant. You want more. You follow or admire the people sitting in the seats of significance you desire to occupy. You become dissatisfied with your life. Never mind that you might be raising the next generation, helping in your church or community, and sharing kind words with strangers you meet. You want more. You focus on the wrong things and forget or miss the opportunities for significance at your fingertips every single day.

Struggle 3—Loss of Significance

Or maybe you've held a seat of significance with great authority and leadership, then God asked you to step away. Sometimes you may look back and feel like what you are doing now doesn't really matter. You want your old seat back.

Here's something to get excited about: God doesn't define significance the way we do. For example, God told Samuel, *"...The Lord doesn't see things the way you see them. People judge by outward appearance, but the Lord looks at the heart."* (1 Samuel 16:7 NLT)

The good news is your significance has never been and will never be defined by others. You may have millions of followers, build a business, or become the president, premier, or leader of a team. Or maybe your significance will come from sharing a kind word with a stranger, your spouse, or your child. Perhaps you will shape minds in a classroom, bake for your neighbors, or simply produce excellent work on your job every day.

You don't have to "do" something significant to be significant. You're important simply because you exist. When you get out of your head and redefine significance from "being" important to the act of "doing" something important in service to God and your fellow man, you'll find opportunities for significance everywhere.

Prayer

Dear Heavenly Father,

    I sometimes wonder if what I'm doing matters. I wonder if I matter. Sometimes I feel small and insignificant. Help me to let go of my desire for significance so I can live the life of significance You have planned for me, whatever that is. No more, no less.

    Amen.

8

IT WAS NEVER WHAT WE WERE TOLD ANYWAY

HOW MIGHT BELIEVING THAT GOD IS IN YOUR
TRIBE TRANSFORM YOUR CONFIDENCE?

*"God replied to Moses, 'I am who I am.'
Say this to the people of Israel:
'I am has sent me to you.'"*
—*Exodus 3:14* NLT

As a coach and former HR executive for over two decades, I've had a front-row seat to the innermost thoughts of thousands of employees, leaders, and women. I've listened to their ambitions, dreams, and fears.

One of the topics that often comes up, especially for women, is showing up with confidence. When I ask most leaders to describe what confidence looks and feels like, they talk about always knowing and being in control. They want to walk into a room and know what to say and do every single time. They want to insulate themselves from the pain of failure or rejection and fear stemming from uncertainty.

Fear and uncertainty are emotions we all experience. One of the most powerful stories of fear and vulnerability in leadership is the story of Moses found in Exodus Chapters 3 and 4. Moses, who is arguably one of the most extraordinary leaders in the Bible, struggled with confidence. In fact, he was so insecure he argued with God five times.

Protest 1

God tells Moses, *"'Now go, for I am sending you to Pharaoh. You must lead my people Israel out of Egypt.' But Moses protested to God, 'Who am I to appear before Pharaoh? Who am I to lead the people of Israel out of Egypt?' God answered, 'I will be with you. And this is your sign that I am the one who has sent you…'" (Exodus 3:10–12 NLT)*

Protest 2

"'…If I go to the people of Israel and tell them, "The God of your ancestors has sent me to you," they will ask me, "What is his name?" Then what should I tell them?' God replied to Moses, 'I am who I am. Say this to the people of Israel: I Am has sent me to you.'" (Exodus 3:13–14 NLT)

Protest 3

"But Moses protested again, 'What if they won't believe me or listen to me? What if they say, "The Lord never appeared to you"?'" (Exodus 4:1 NLT)

Then, God gave Moses three signs to show to Pharoah. The first sign was to turn his staff into a snake. The second sign was that Moses' hand would turn white with leprosy when he put it into his cloak.

Then came the third sign. God said, *"'...And if they don't believe you or listen to you even after these two signs, then take some water from the Nile River and pour it out on the dry ground. When you do, the water from the Nile will turn to blood on the ground.'" (Exodus 4:9 NLT)*

Protest 4

"Moses pleaded with the Lord, 'O Lord, I'm not very good with words. I never have been, and I'm not now, even though you have spoken to me. I get tongue-tied, and my words get tangled.' Then the Lord asked Moses, 'Who makes a person's mouth? Who decides whether people speak or do not speak, hear or do not hear, see or do not see? Is it not I, the Lord? Now go! I will be with you as you speak, and I will instruct you in what to say.'" (Exodus 4:10–12 NLT)

Protest 5

Even after all that, Moses pleaded again with God, *"...Lord, please! Send anyone else." (Exodus 4:13 NLT)*

At this point, God became angry and told him, "Go! Your brother will help you."

Have you ever felt like Moses? I know I have. But I believe that we have misunderstood confidence. So, what is confidence?

While most dictionaries commonly define confidence as certainty, when all is said and done, what can we really be certain of 100 percent of the time? I've found that instead of certainty, confidence is about moving forward, acting, and trusting that we can figure "it" out with our hands in God's.

My definition: Confidence is the belief that as life shifts, we can figure it out.

Like Moses, we'll never have all the necessary skills and knowledge to tackle the things life places in our path. Like Moses, we'll encounter unknowns, difficulties, and challenging people. Like Moses, sometimes we'll max out and won't have the physical or emotional capacity to do more, and we need support.

The beautiful thing is we can be confident because God is a part of our tribe. The same promises God made to Moses belong to you as God's child:

- ∞ I will be with you.
- ∞ I am sending you.
- ∞ I can perform miracles.
- ∞ I will give you the words to say.
- ∞ Go. I'll send a tribe to help you.

We can walk in confidence because we know God will move heaven and earth to give us what is best for us. We can also be confident even if the answer is no. When the no's come, if we believe in God and what He says, we can accept the answer in peace, knowing He will withhold no good thing (Psalms 84:11 NIV) and wants to take care of His children (Matthew 6:26–34 NIV).

Fear is a feeling we all feel. That is why God inspired the Bible's writers to pen "fear not" 365 times. The feeling of fear is normal. Ultimately, it's the decisions we make after the feeling that matter. So Be Different. Live your life. Move forward, and trust that God will work everything out for your good. Because, you see, confidence was never what we were told, anyway.

Prayer

Dear Father,

    At different times, I've felt You leading me down a path. However, like Moses, sometimes I struggle. Even knowing all You've done in the past, I still struggle with fear. Fear of failure and fear of rejection. God, I know fear doesn't come from You. As I make plans, show me if what I want to do isn't in Your plan. It could be through Your word, a whisper from the Holy Spirit, someone from my tribe, or any other way You choose! Because I don't want to take one step in a direction You didn't design. I leave this moment, comforted by Your promise that You'll always be with me even until the end of the earth. Here I am, ready to move in confidence, knowing You're in control and have given me everything I need for this time.

    Amen.

9

REMEMBER THE LION AND THE BEAR

WHAT VOICES DO YOU NEED TO QUIET?
WHAT PAST VICTORIES CAN
YOU REMEMBER?

"I have done this to both lions and bears, and I'll do it to this pagan Philistine, too, for he has defied the armies of the living God!"
—1 Samuel 17:36 NLT

As you already know, I took a leap from corporate executive to entrepreneur several years ago. Even though I come from a family of entrepreneurs, I didn't fully appreciate or anticipate the magnitude of the change. Moving from the certainty of a paycheck, resources, and a team to doing it all on my own was exciting and intimidating all at the same time!

About a year into my journey, I spoke with a friend who was a former pastor about my experience, and he said, "You're not the only one.

I've learned more about faith through my entrepreneurship journey than I did in all my years as a pastor."

Like entrepreneurship, life can be a roller coaster of ups and downs. One moment, we've got it under control, and then the next, something comes out of left field that causes us to doubt our path. I love the story of David because his life was full of uncertainty. One moment, he was anointed king; the next, he was playing his harp while the king threw spears at him. Another day, he was marrying the king's daughter; the next, he fled for his life and hid in caves. One moment, his family was at peace, and the next, his sons were killing each other. Through it all, David's faith in God remained strong despite the ups and downs. But how?

David's faith stayed strong because he chose to remember.

Step back in time with me to 1 Samuel 17. The Philistines had decided it was time to go to war, and Saul had gathered his troops on a hill near the valley of Elah. Every day, the Philistine champion Goliath would come out and taunt them. He was over nine feet tall, and his armor was so heavy his iron spearhead weighed fifteen pounds! Every day for forty days, he mocked the army of Israel and their God. He was formidable. Whenever the Israelites saw Goliath, they fled from him in great fear.

David's brothers were with Saul in the valley of Elah. Their father, Jesse, sent David with a basket of food and instructions to come back with a report on how they were doing. David arrived at the camp, and as he talked to his brothers, Goliath came out to shout his daily disrespectful taunt. David was amazed to see the army of

God running and started to ask questions: "What will a man get for killing this giant? Who is he to defy God anyway?"

Someone reported David's questions back to the king, so Saul sent for him. During their conversation, *"'Don't worry about this Philistine,' David told Saul. 'I'll go fight him!' 'Don't be ridiculous!' Saul replied. 'There's no way you can fight this Philistine and possibly win! You're only a boy, and he's been a man of war since his youth.'" (1 Samuel 17:32–33 NLT)*

> *But David persisted. "I have been taking care of my father's sheep and goats," he said. "When a lion or a bear comes to steal a lamb from the flock, I go after it with a club and rescue the lamb from its mouth. If the animal turns on me, I catch it by the jaw and club it to death. I have done this to both lions and bears, and I'll do it to this pagan Philistine, too, for he has defied the armies of the living God!" (1 Samuel 17:34–36 NLT)*

All of us, at different times, will face the giants of life. No matter where you are or how you feel, remember you have access to the same God who protected David. He wants to do the same for you. Like David, there are a few actions you can take if your faith is fading and you start to feel doubt:

Quiet the Voices

On the way to the fight, David probably thought about all the voices: the voices of fear from the other Israelites; the voices of rebuke from his brothers, who questioned his motives; and the voice of King Saul, who told him he was too young. He might have even had to contend with the voice in his own head telling him Goliath was too big. If you're in a battle, I can almost guarantee you'll be met with voices that will tell you, "You can't." When that happens, remember the only voice that matters is the voice of God.

Remember the Past

David was confident he would win because he remembered how God had helped him defeat the lions and bears of his past. Like David, you're positioned for victory. Like David, you can quiet the voices, take your position, and remember how God has helped you fight the battles of your past. Pause for just a moment and look back over your life. How has God shown up? What amazing things has He done in your life and the lives of those around you? God doesn't change, He doesn't lie, and His love is constant. Even when you have experienced pain, if you look back, you'll see the pain was for your protection or to propel you into purpose.

Take Your Position

When David inquired about Goliath, it would've been perfectly reasonable and rational to turn around and run. He was, after all, very young and not skilled in warfare. But his belief in the power of God propelled him to ask questions, pick up stones on his way to do battle, and then take his position for the fight. Like David, we can trust God and move forward in faith. Like David, we can say, "The Lord is my rock, my fortress and my deliverer; my God is my rock, in whom I take refuge, my shield and the horn of my salvation, my stronghold." (Psalms 18:2 NIV)

I know I want to live with the faith and courage of David. Don't you?

When you face your battles, don't look at the size of the giant. Quiet the voices. Remember how God has protected you when you've faced the lions and bears of your past, and then take your position and watch what God will do!

Prayer

Dear God,

    I want to say thank You for all the times You have rescued me from the giants of my life. I'm grateful for all the times You protected, promoted, and pivoted me from attacks I couldn't see. God, it's so easy for me to get stuck or grow paralyzed. The world, with all its divides, pain, and unexpected atrocities, is enough to stop me in my tracks. But I know I'm on assignment. I ask You, when I struggle with my faith or believe I don't have what it takes to move forward, help me quiet the voices, remember how You have shown up in the past, and then take my position. Just like David.

    Amen.

10

WHY ME, WHY NOW?

IN WHAT WAYS HAS GOD USED YOUR PAST PAIN AS PREPARATION?

"But Joseph said to them, 'Don't be afraid. Am I in the place of God? You intended to harm me, but God intended it for good to accomplish what is now being done, the saving of many lives.'"
—Genesis 50:19–20 NIV

It was sports day! As the sun poked its head out from below the horizon and began to rise, I felt that familiar sense of anxious anticipation in my stomach. Today was going to be different. Let me give you some history. Back in her day, my mom was a track star before she decided to settle down and start a family.

However, her love for sprinting never left her. My mom did her best to pass her passion for running on to her kids. I was at the front of the line! I loved running. I loved sports day.

Leading up to sports day, my mom trained us and showed us the techniques of her craft. She loved running so much that she entered the parents race at the end of every sports day.

For our entire elementary and high school careers, she never lost once. To give you some context, there are four of us kids. We attended our school for more than a combined twenty years, and she never lost once! Many years later, when my kids started school, she continued to run. Year after year, like clockwork, almost every year Nana would win.

However, this year was different. My mom was overseas. I was down thirty pounds and in the best shape I had been in since my kids were born. This year, I was going to run my own parents race!

I lined up with the other parents. Almost every single one looked younger than me. Palms sweaty and adrenaline pumping, I waited for the whistle. Not looking to the left or right, I took off. This was it! I could feel that old familiar feeling come back as my body began to pick up speed. I settled into a comfortable stride as I led the pack, when suddenly I felt something crack in my foot as I stumbled over the finish line.

I'd never broken anything! Seriously! Not a bone or a finger. Never. My foot began to swell and the pain set in. In the days that followed, I tried to make sense of it all. I silently asked God, "Why me, why now?"

"Why, after all these years?"

"Why, when I'm in such great shape?"

"Why would you let this happen now when I need to move to stay healthy?"

"Why, when I have so much to do and so many things to take care of?"

"Why me, why now?"

The days passed, and I couldn't get that thought out of my head. During my devotion time, I was led to study the book of Genesis and the story of Joseph. Throughout his life, Joseph experienced many "why me, why now" moments.

The Rejected

When Joseph was a young boy, the Bible says, his father loved him more than any of his other sons. From time to time, Joseph reported to his father some of the bad things his brothers were doing (Genesis 37:2). As a result, his brothers hated him and rarely said a kind word to him. Growing up in that kind of environment had to be tough. In his most vulnerable moments, I imagine he might have asked God, "Why don't they love me? Why me, why now?"

The Unloved

Joseph also dreamed dreams. When he told his brothers about them, the Bible says, these dreams incensed them and they hated him even more. Can you imagine him saying to himself, "Why don't they love me? Why are they so angry about a simple dream?"

The Slave

One day, Jacob sent Joseph to see how his brothers and the sheep were faring. When Joseph arrived, his brothers ripped off the beautiful robe he was wearing and threw him into an empty hole in the ground (Genesis 37:24). Can you imagine Joseph saying, "Why me, why now? Why are they treating me this way?" Only he didn't realize it was about to get a whole lot worse. He was sold into slavery (Genesis 37:28). At this point, wouldn't you have been almost inconsolable? "God, why me? Why now?"

The Accused

Joseph arrived in Egypt and was sold into slavery. He did his best to honor his master as if unto God. However, after some time, his master's wife accused Joseph of attempting to force himself on her (Genesis 39:14), and Joseph was thrown into prison. Can you imagine him crying out to God, "Why me, why now?"

The Forgotten

It would have been easy to be bitter, but once again, Joseph worked as if unto God. While in prison, he met Pharaoh's baker and cupbearer and interpreted their dreams. All Joseph asked the cupbearer in return was to remember him and mention his name to Pharaoh so he might let Joseph out of prison. But the cupbearer forgot (Genesis 40:14). As the days stretched into months and months into years, can you imagine him crying to God, "Why me, why now?"

I'm sure that, like Joseph, at some point in your life, you have experienced your own "why me, why now" moments at the hands of people. Perhaps it started as a child when you were rejected by a parent or classmates on the playground. Maybe you suffered mental or physical abuse at the hands of someone who was supposed to love or protect you. Your "why me, why now" moment could even have come in the form of being overlooked at work because of bias or being let go when your company restructured.

God sees you and understands your pain. For years, Joseph suffered extraordinary pain. He was rejected, unloved, made a slave, accused, and forgotten. But that's not the end of his story. Joseph went on to take another name:

The Ruler

When God's timing was right, Joseph was promoted to second-in-command over the entire nation of Egypt (Genesis 41:41). When it happened, he was ready. His many years of painful "why me, why now" moments were not punishment but preparation.

No matter the pain you have suffered at the hands of others, God wants you to know He is still here and loves you. My prayer for you is that you can release all your "why me, why now" moments to Him and, like Joseph, declare, "You intended to harm me, but God intended it for good."

Prayer

Dear Heavenly Father,

For too long, the pain I've experienced at the hands of others has consumed my soul and mind. God, it has stopped me, stifled me, and caused me to doubt. I ask You to help me trust you. Help me move past my pain into the plan I know You have for me. God, help me, like Joseph, to see and believe that my "why me, why now" moments were never about them and that You will work it *all* for my good.

Amen.

11

STUCK IN A CYCLE

WHAT STEPS DO YOU NEED TO TAKE TO STOP
COMPARING YOURSELF TO OTHERS?

*"When the Lord saw that Leah was unloved,
He enabled her to have children, but
Rachel could not conceive."*
—Genesis 29:31 NLT

When I was about fifteen, my mom gave me a book titled *Leah* by Lois N. Erickson. Immediately, I was intrigued. First, the title was my name, but the subtitle—"a love story"—puzzled me. Based on everything I knew, Leah's story was definitely not about love, so I read. In fact, I've read that book at least two dozen times, maybe more. The cover is ripped and tattered. Now it's so old the pages have started to turn brown.

Erickson had a gift for making the characters come alive in my young mind. As I turned the pages, I could feel the soft fabric draped on Leah's skin as she shopped in the market or the grime caking her feet as she walked the dusty roads looking for her father. I could almost taste the meals she cooked in her pots, waiting for her boys and Jacob to come home to eat. However, even more than the imagery, Erickson had a fantastic ability to capture the characters' emotions.

If you're unfamiliar with the story or need a refresher, you'll find it in Genesis Chapters 29 and 30. Leah was the older sister with weak eyes, and no one wanted to marry her. Jacob was madly in love with her younger sister, Rachel, and worked seven years just to marry her. However, Leah's father, Laban, arranged for Leah to take Rachel's place on the wedding day. Jacob was furious, and Rachel was heartbroken. Laban quickly gave Rachel to Jacob as well. Can you imagine waiting all your life to be married only to be rejected by your husband because he really wanted someone else?

Laban's lie started a comparison cycle that plagued the two sisters most of their lives. Leah compared herself to Rachel's beauty and the fact that Rachel so effortlessly commanded all of Jacob's love. Rachel, on the other hand, compared her barrenness to Leah's ability to give Jacob sons. It was a painful situation: stuck sisters, each desperately wanting what the other had.

Perhaps from time to time, you have found yourself stuck in a cycle of comparison. Maybe it looks like this:

You wanted that job, but she got it, along with all the money and perks that came with it. What you can't see are the long hours and sacrificed time with family. While you yearn for her job, she cries to God to be home with her kids at night. Perhaps she thinks you're stunning and looks at your social media profile with envy. But she can't see the crushing pressure you feel to look and be a certain way all the time. You want her seemingly wonderful life, but what you can't see is her failing marriage or silent illness. We can't see, so we stay stuck, comparing, unable to see what's on the other side.

As I read and reread the story of Leah, I often wondered why my mom named me Leah. Why name me after the sister who was considered unattractive and whose name means weary? Why name me after the sister who spent so much of her life unloved and lonely?

The more I think about it, I believe she was onto something because I found two powerful lessons in the story of Leah that can give us hope when we get stuck in a cycle of comparison.

God Sees You

Genesis 29:31 (NLT) says, *"When the Lord saw that Leah was unloved, he enabled her to have children…"* Leah's story reminds us that God listens to the hearts of His children. Like Leah, God sees you and understands your pain and has a plan for you. It may not be what you want, but I promise He will give you exactly what you need.

Praise Through the Pain

We can understand the depth of Leah's pain because Genesis 29:32–35 (NLT) reveals her words after the birth of her first three sons. After Reuben was born, she said, *"'The Lord has noticed my misery, and now my husband will love me.'"* After Simeon, she said, *"'The Lord heard that I was unloved and has given me another son.'"* After Levi, she said, *"'Surely this time my husband will feel affection for me, since I have given him three sons!'"*

I don't know about you, but I feel for Leah. To love a man, have his children, and still be rejected must have hurt.

However, she did something different after the birth of her fourth son, Judah. She said, "Now I will praise the Lord." *(Genesis 29:35 NLT)*

I don't know where you're stuck. In this moment, please remember that you don't have to stay stuck in the comparison cycle. Leah's story reminds us our path to breaking the cycle is to remember that God sees us and then praise Him. Unloved Leah was not as beautiful. Unloved Leah was neglected and hurt. Unloved Leah was blessed by God with children. Unloved Leah chose to praise God through her pain. Unloved Leah became the mother of Judah, and from the tribe of Judah, Jesus, the savior of the world, was born. And it's this same Unloved Leah whose sons' names are written on the gates of heaven (Revelation 21:12).

As painful as it was, the story of Leah is indeed a love story. However, it's not a story of a man loving a woman, but the story of God loving a woman so much He heard her cry, answered her cry, and then positioned her to be the very vessel through which He would save the world.

You never have to and never need to compare yourself to anyone else. You matter too much to God for that. In those moments when you get stuck comparing yourself to others, ask God to help you turn your pain into praise, and then step back and watch God turn your praise into purpose. If He did it for Leah, He'll do it for you too.

Prayer

Dear God,

    I get stuck in the comparison cycle more often than I should. When I consider all You've done and all You've given me, I know I shouldn't compare, but I still get stuck. God, thank you for reminding me through the story of Leah that my feelings are valid and that I matter to You. God, it's not easy to praise through everything that life sends my way. Please help me praise You in my pain and then step back and watch as You turn my praise into purpose.

    Amen.

12

GOOD ENOUGH

HOW CAN YOU MOVE FORWARD USING THE STRENGTHS AND GIFTS YOU HAVE?

"'But Lord,' Gideon replied, 'how can I rescue Israel? My clan is the weakest in the whole tribe of Manasseh, and I am the least in my entire family!'"
—Judges 6:15 NLT

In my line of work, I often receive requests from people asking me to do new things. On one occasion, I received a message from an organization asking me to facilitate a session with their executive team. It was a big, multibillion-dollar company. I knew I could deliver on the work. Yet, my brain still wanted to protect me from failure. Immediately I began to think about all the reasons why I couldn't do it. Have you ever experienced imposter syndrome? That feeling of knowing you can do something, but a voice inside says you can't or you're not good enough?

Come back in time with me to Judges Chapter 6. Things weren't going well for the Israelites. Once again, they had done evil in the sight of the Lord. Consequently, the Lord allowed the Midianites to destroy their crops and take all their cattle until nothing was left, leading them to face starvation. With no other recourse, they cried out to God for help.

The Bible says an angel of the Lord came and sat beneath the great tree at Ophrah, where he found Gideon and said to him, "... 'Mighty hero, the Lord is with you!'" (Judges 6:12 NLT)

Up to this point in his life, Gideon had done nothing to make him a hero. In fact, on the day the angel visited, he was at the bottom of a wine press threshing wheat. Threshing is the process of separating the edible part of the grain from the inedible husk.

The process involves spreading the grain on the threshing floor for horses or oxen to trample. After the grains are loose, they're beaten by hand. So there Gideon was. Probably hot and sweaty, beating grain in the bottom of a hole. Nothing seems heroic about that!

> "Sir," Gideon replied, "if the Lord is with us, why has all this happened to us? And where are all the miracles our ancestors told us about? Didn't they say, 'The Lord brought us up out of Egypt'? But now the Lord has abandoned us and handed us over to the Midianites."
>
> Then the Lord turned to him and said, "Go with the strength you have and rescue Israel from the Midianites. I am sending you!"
>
> "But Lord," Gideon replied, "how can I rescue Israel? My clan is the weakest in the whole tribe of Manasseh, and I am the least in my entire family!"

The Lord said to him, "I will be with you. And you will destroy the Midianites as if you were fighting against one man." (Judges 6:13–16 NLT)

There are a few powerful lessons in this exchange:

God Sees You Differently

The angel greeted Gideon with the words "mighty hero." The angel didn't address Gideon based on his current activity as a farmer threshing wheat. No. He spoke to him based on who God had created him to be.

You Have Everything You Need

When Gideon shared the dire situation the Israelites were in with God, the Lord told him, "Go with the strength you have." When Gideon reminded God of all his weaknesses, God reassured him, saying, "I *will* be with you, and you *will* be victorious." Gideon didn't need anything more than exactly who he was to rescue the Israelites from their enemies.

Gideon became a judge, fought many against-all-odds battles, and ensured peace in the land for about forty years.

Like Gideon, you have a purpose, and God is calling you to more. If there are moments when you don't feel smart enough, wise enough, rich enough, connected enough, or [fill in your blank] enough, it's okay. On those days, you can claim God's promise to Gideon: "I *will* be with you, and you *will* be victorious!"

God has meticulously placed everything you need inside you. He made you, He called you, and I pray this reading reminds you that whenever and wherever He sends you, you'll always be good enough.

Prayer

> Dear Heavenly Father,
>
> More often than I'd like, the voice in my head tells me that I can't. Thank you for stopping by and reminding me I have everything I need to impact this world. Thank You for reminding me I'll always be good enough to do what You have called me to do.
>
> Amen.

13

RAISE THE BAR

WHERE MIGHT GOD BE CALLING YOU TO INFLUENCE CHANGE?

"Barak said to her, 'If you go with me, I will go; but if you don't go with me, I won't go.'"
—Judges 4:8 NIV

When I was in high school, I had an addiction. I *loved* basketball. Even though I couldn't play, I adored the game. I spent countless hours watching games and organizing watch parties. My passion for the game ran so deep I even cooked breakfast to encourage my brothers and their friends to wake up and play every Sunday, so I could watch them in action. And that's saying something, because cooking is not my favorite pastime! Over the years, as my life and schedule changed, I stopped watching the sport regularly. Nonetheless, from time to time, I still enjoy a good sports movie or documentary, especially if it involves a comeback.

A few years ago, Netflix released the story of the US men's basketball team's mission to win a gold medal at the 2008 Olympics in Beijing.[2] Initially, you couldn't call them a team. They were talented players with big egos. They tell the story of getting dressed and going out to party the night away. After a long night, they returned to the hotel in the early morning hours to find Kobe Bryant on his way to work out at the gym. They looked at each other and asked, "Is he for real?" The next day, LeBron James and Dwyane Wade made their way to the gym at 5:00 a.m. Soon, the entire team was up early, working out and connecting. Kobe's focus on the mission and his presence shifted the team's work ethic, leading them to win gold.

We find a similar story of raising the bar in Judges Chapter 4. At the time, Deborah, a prophet, was leading Israel.

> *She sent for Barak, son of Abinoam from Kedesh in Naphtali and said to him, "The Lord, the God of Israel, commands you: 'Go, take with you ten thousand men of Naphtali and Zebulun and lead them up to Mount Tabor. I will lead Sisera, the commander of Jabin's army, with his chariots and his troops to the Kishon River and give him into your hands.'"*
>
> *Barak said to her, "If you go with me, I will go; but if you don't go with me, I won't go."*
>
> *"Certainly I will go with you," said Deborah. "But because of the course you are taking, the honor will not be yours, for the Lord will deliver Sisera into the hands of a woman…" (Judges 4:6–9 NIV)*

What are a few takeaways we can find in the stories of Kobe and Deborah?

Your Presence Can Raise the Bar

When he accepted the invitation to join the Olympic team, Kobe understood the mission. The Americans had invented basketball, but due to complacency, they allowed the rest of the world to mature and beat them at their own game. Kobe realized it was time for the US team to raise the bar, and his presence transformed his teammates' focus.

Your Presence Can Change Outcomes

Similarly, the people of Israel had become arrogant and done evil in God's eyes, leading to their enslavement. They cried out to God, who heard them and chose Barak to lead them to deliverance. Yet Barak was afraid and asked Deborah to lead the army. Her God-centered, fearless presence gave Barak and the army the confidence to move forward and defeat the enemy.

As we conclude this pillar—Trust Different—remember the power God gives you to choose. Every day you can shrink back like Barak, leaving God's work to others, or you can step up like Kobe and Deborah and be an agent of change. Today is a new beginning, a day filled with endless possibilities and another chance to trust who God created you to be and raise the bar.

Prayer

Dear Heavenly Father,

I know You have a plan for me. Yet, with frustrating frequency, I slide down the mountain of courage into the valley of doubt. I know I have a purpose, but occasionally, with the enemy waiting at every corner, I still struggle with worry and fear. God, I'm asking You to remind me I can make a difference in those moments. Just being and living as who You created me to be will impact lives and situations. Take me, mold me, use me, and allow my presence to raise the bar.

Amen!

Reflect & Renew

Living and walking confidently in the peace of who God created us to be is no easy task. As we wrap up this second pillar—Trust Different—take a few moments to reflect on the questions we have explored in our journey so far. Ask God to show you where He wants you to grow.

LISTEN DIFFERENT

1. Is it time to pause and listen for God's direction in your busy life?
2. How can you be more intentional about finding or creating space to pause?
3. Have you asked God to help you live out His plan for your life? If not, why?
4. What tribes do you have or need to build?

TRUST DIFFERENT

5. In what ways can you lean on God to help you fight and win your battles?
6. How might adopting the way God sees you impact your life?
7. What steps could you take to believe in your value even when you're not doing something big?

⑧ How might believing that God is in your tribe transform your confidence?

⑨ What voices do you need to quiet? What past victories can you remember?

⑩ In what ways has God used your past pain as preparation?

⑪ What steps do you need to take to stop comparing yourself to others?

⑫ How can you move forward using the strengths and gifts you have?

⑬ Where might God be calling you to influence change?

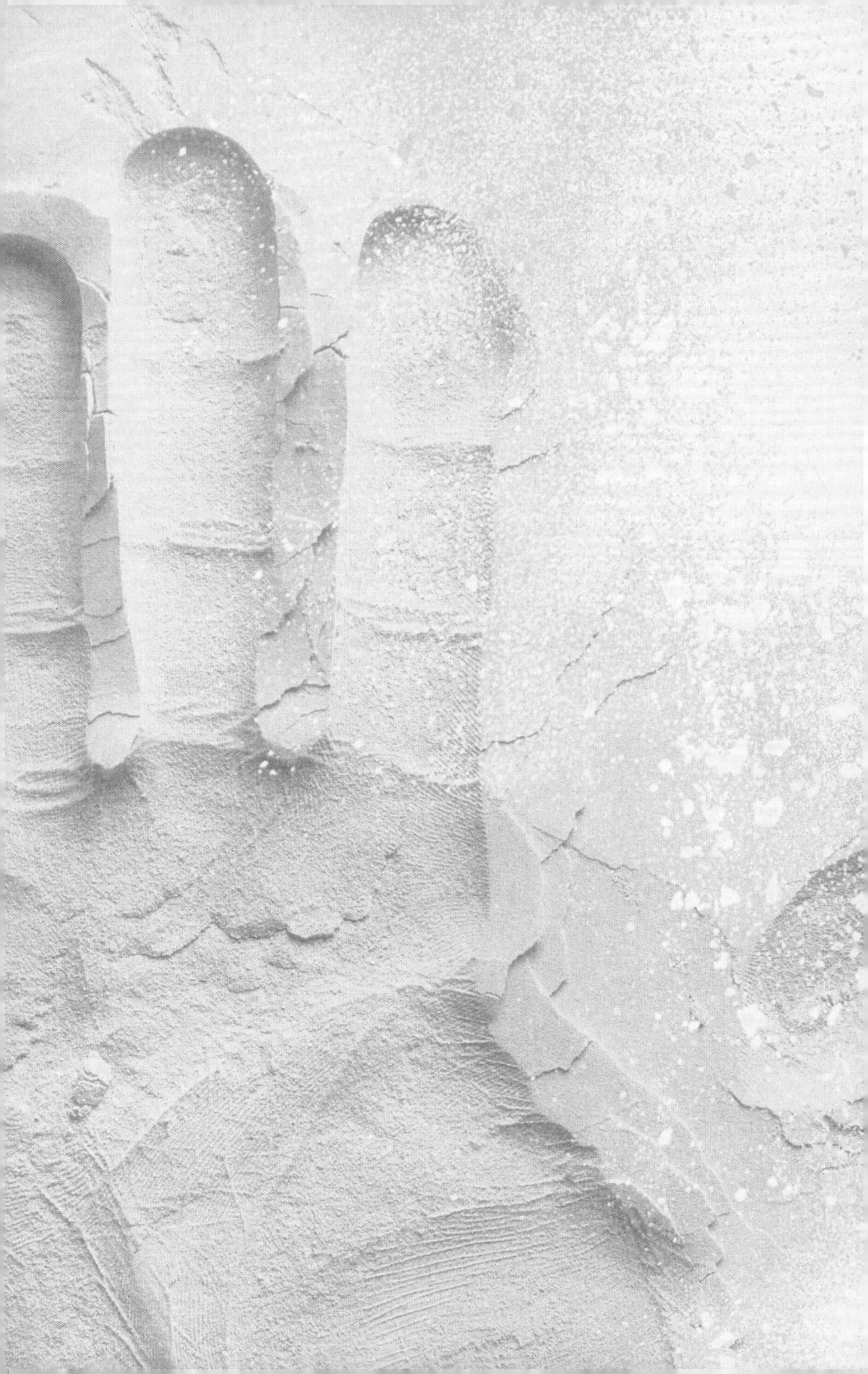

Think DIFFERENT

PILLAR THREE

Think Different

Based on the title of this pillar, you might be thinking the next few chapters will focus on mindset. They do, but not in the way you might expect. If you think about it, when you're up at night or days on end struggling with a relationship or situation, where does the majority of the struggle take place? You guessed it: in your mind.

Welcome to Pillar Three: Think Different. If we want to be God's hands on earth, this pillar invites us to quiet the voice in our head and examine the relationship expectations we have of others. Are you ready to get to work?

The mind is the CEO of our lives. Where it leads, we follow.

Change your thoughts and change your life.

14

THE ULTIMATUMS

HOW CAN YOU CHOOSE LOVE AND
PRACTICE PEACE DAILY?

*"And so we know and rely on the love
God has for us. God is love. Whoever lives
in love lives in God, and God in them.
This is how love is made complete
among us so that we will have
confidence on the day of judgment:
In this world we are like Jesus."*
—1 John 4:16–17 NIV

As you may recall from Chapter 4, when I started writing my first book, *Assemble the Tribe*, I was invited to speak at a church, but it never happened. While preparing for that speaking engagement, I came across this devotional's text. Honestly, it instilled a bit of fear in me because it felt like an ultimatum. Was the text really saying if I couldn't put aside my pain, anger, and frustrations and choose to love, there's no way I could be confident that heaven would be my final home?

During my studies I ran across a second text: *"Pursue peace with all people, and holiness, without which no one will see the Lord." (Hebrews 12:14 NKJV)*. Doesn't that feel like another ultimatum, and a really serious one at that?

The Greek word for peace in this text is *eiréné*, meaning quietness, rest, and peace of mind.[3] *Eiréné* comes from the word *eirō*, which means to join together into a whole or wholeness. And wholeness occurs when all essential parts are joined together.

Over the years, as I've studied and experienced the love of God, I've come to realize that, depending on the state of our hearts, these texts could be gentle, wise instructions or uncompromising demands. They remind us that the goal is to continually strive to become more like Christ every single day, and bring *eiréné,* (wholeness) to our homes, work, and community. So how might *eiréné* practically show up in our lives?

It was a last-minute invitation. There was so much to do. I could've easily spent a few more hours in the office, but I decided to shut down the computer and spend the evening with my friends watching the Oscar-nominated film *Hidden Figures*. This film tells the story of three women, Katherine Johnson, Dorothy Vaughan, and Mary Jackson, who worked as mathematicians and engineers at NASA during the space race to the moon in the 1960s. While each woman's perseverance in the face of sexism and racism is remarkable, I found myself drawn to the story of Dorothy Vaughan (played by Octavia Spencer).

Dorothy was a "human computer," which is a term used to describe a person who performed complex mathematical calculations manually before computers. She was brilliant. But she was continually overlooked for promotion, forced instead to train her white colleagues, who were promoted above her. What I admire about Dorothy is that despite having every right to be angry, difficult, or frustrated, she chose peace, performed her job with excellence, and focused on teaching herself and her team to program the newly introduced IBM computers. Her determination secured their positions at NASA and ushered in a new era of computer programming. Her choice to peacefully focus on progress positively impacted the lives of every person on her team, likely benefitting their families for generations to come.[4]

Like Dorothy, have you ever been wounded by someone and as a result struggled to pursue peace and love? I believe the two texts in this reading are clear ultimatums. But how can we experience peace of mind or bring wholeness and love when people are complicated, unkind, or downright evil?

About now, you might be thinking about the person or situation that challenges your last nerve! They have wounded or hurt you so badly you struggle to pursue peace and love. Don't worry. Many believers I talk to often equate loving others and pursuing peace with simply being "nice." Dorothy Vaughan's story reminds us that peace doesn't mean being a pushover. It's about focusing less on the challenge and more on the choice. It's about taking control of your thought life and choosing how you will show up in the face the people challenges that life will throw your way.

The reality is, even when we make the choice to love and pursue peace, because people are so complicated, sometimes we will fail.

The good news is that God understands, and He promises in Lamentations 3:22–23 to not only be compassionate and merciful, but to renew His mercy every morning. Even if we stumbled in showing love or seeking peace yesterday, today offers a fresh opportunity to try again.

Over the next few chapters, in this new pillar—Think Different—we'll ask God to help you change your thought life so you can bring peace and wholeness to people and situations wherever you go. Our Bible readings (1 John 4:16–17 & Hebrews 12:14) and Dorothy Vaughan's story remind us we have so much to gain in this world and the next when we do.

Prayer

> Dear Father,
>
> I try to be a good person. It seems like from one thought or interaction to the next, I don't do enough to love and bring wholeness to those around me. Thank You for the promise that You'll be merciful when I struggle and fail. There are people You need me to reach and lives You need me to touch, so I accept Your ultimatums and commit to doing my best to love and pursue peace wherever I go.
> Amen.

15

THE GOD GIFT

WHAT THOUGHTS OR FEELINGS ABOUT PEOPLE MIGHT YOU NEED TO LET GO?

"'As surely as the Lord your God lives,' she replied, 'I don't have any bread— only a handful of flour in a jar and a little olive oil in a jug. I am gathering a few sticks to take home and make a meal for myself and my son, that we may eat it—and die.'"
—1 Kings 17:12 NIV

"I'm so angry!" she exclaimed. "For years, I've given! I've sacrificed my needs, time, and money. Even after all that, I feel left out, forgotten, and unappreciated. How could they! Take and take and then forget me!"

As we talked, I could feel the bitterness and pain filtering through the airwaves of the call. However, as we started to pull the pieces of her story apart, we found deep underlying feelings of hurt, pain, and rejection.

Has this ever been you?

On the pages of 1 Kings 16 and 17, we find a beautiful example of giving at great sacrifice. Ahab was king. The Bible says King Ahab did more to provoke the anger of the Lord, the God of Israel, than any of the other kings of Israel before him. God sent the prophet Elijah to tell King Ahab that a drought was coming. No dew or rain would touch Israel until Elijah gave the word.

After Elijah delivered the message to Ahab, God instructed him to go to a brook where the ravens would bring him bread and meat each morning and evening. But after a while the brook dried up. There was no rainfall anywhere on the land. God told Elijah to go to the village of Zarephath, where He had instructed a widow to feed Elijah. When Elijah arrived at the town's gates and saw the widow collecting sticks, he asked her, *"...Would you bring me a little water in a jar so I may have a drink?" As she was going to get it, he called, "And bring me, please, a piece of bread."* (1Kings 17: 10-11)

The widow paused, looked up at Elijah, and said, *"'As surely as the Lord your God lives...I don't have any bread—only a handful of flour in a jar and a little olive oil in a jug. I am gathering a few sticks to take home and make a meal for myself and my son, that we may eat it—and die.'"* (1 Kings 17:12 NIV)

For just a moment, pretend you're the widow. In biblical times, women were under the authority and protection of their husbands.

But now she is all alone and has no one to help provide for her and her son during this terrible drought. The widow has done everything in her power to protect her son. She has rationed their food and even gone hungry. Now she is outside in the punishing heat, thirsty, sweaty, exhausted, picking up sticks to make her last meal before she dies. Then along comes this grown, capable, seemingly well-fed man, asking her for something to eat. I don't know about you, but taking food from my son to feed Elijah would be the last thing I'd want to do.

Perhaps you know the story: Elijah tells her not to worry. He tells her that if she feeds him, God will provide for her and she will always have enough flour and oil until it rains again. I'm sure she was hesitant, but she did as Elijah asked and gave him her last bit of food to eat.

True to Elijah's word, for the remainder of the famine there was always enough for the widow and her son to eat. Sometime later, the widow's son became sick and died. Her only son, the son she loved, the son who was to become her protector, was dead!

In her grief, she said to Elijah, *"'...O man of God, what have you done to me? Have you come here to point out my sins and kill my son?'"* (1 Kings 17:18 NLT)

Elijah took her son in his arms and carried him to his room. He prayed and cried out to the Lord to restore the child. God heard Elijah's prayer and raised the child from the dead, and Elijah returned him to his mother. Then the woman told Elijah, *"'Now I know for sure that you're a man of God, and that the Lord truly speaks through you.'" (1 Kings 17:24 NLT)* Think about that. At the beginning of the story, when she gave Elijah her last bit of food, she was not 100 percent sure who he was, but she gave it anyway. It was this life-or-death sacrifice of obedience that opened God's hand to restore her food pantry and later restore her son's life!

The widow's story reminds us to shift our thinking. Giving is not about good feelings or repeated thank-yous. Giving allows us to be God's hands on earth. We give because God loves a cheerful giver (2 Corinthians 9:7) and it pleases Him (Hebrews 13:15–16). When we please God, not only will He supply our immediate needs, like the widow's, but He'll supply future needs we can't see coming.

I get excited when I think about that. How does this promise make you feel?

You see, God doesn't need you or me to accomplish His plans, but He is kind and loving enough to invite us to share His love with others. Then, He promises us access to abundant gifts above anything we can ask or think (Ephesians 3:20). Sacrificial giving is never easy, and sometimes we may need to build boundaries, but that's a thought for another time.

Elijah's story is a gentle reminder: We can shift how we think instead of getting stuck in pain and disappointment. When all is said and done, our gift isn't in the giving. Our real gift is God.

Prayer

Dear Heavenly Father,

I come to You because, at times, this has been me. I'm excited about giving and hurt when my gifts aren't appreciated or are rejected. God, I'm human, and You made me to feel. In the moments when I'm hurt or disappointed, change my thinking. Help me to remember that appreciation is not the gift; my real gift is You. Thank You for the many times You've allowed me to be Your hands to show others Your love. I release my hurt and give thanks for Your many promises to show up for me in ways I can't even imagine!

Amen.

16

A MESSY TRIBE

WHAT MESSINESS IN YOUR TRIBE MIGHT YOU NEED TO LET IN?

"These are the twelve he appointed: Simon (to whom he gave the name Peter), James son of Zebedee and his brother John (to whom he gave the name Boanerges, which means 'sons of thunder'), Andrew, Philip, Bartholomew, Matthew, Thomas, James son of Alphaeus, Thaddaeus, Simon the Zealot, and Judas Iscariot, who betrayed him."
—Mark 3:16–19 NIV

When I ask most audiences what a tribe is, they often describe it as "my support system, my most trusted advisors, my crew, my mates, aces, my girls, or my people."

I believe tribes are individually complex people who choose to come together to create relationship—which means, sometimes it's going to get messy!

In my work, I advocate for having multiple tribes at different times in our lives. People often ask me: What should I do if I've outgrown my tribe? How will I know when it's time to move on? I often challenge them by asking: Do you really need to move on, or do you need to think differently about the role they play in your life?

Just because people are messy and may not change as we grow doesn't mean they have no value.

We see one of the most profound examples of a messy tribe in the Gospels. When Jesus was ready to begin His ministry, one of the first things He did was assemble a tribe. If I were Christ, on the doorstep of what was to be the culmination of my life's work, I would have looked for people who understood the Bible and prophecy. I might have also included friends who understood my history and who I knew without a shadow of a doubt would always have my back. I might've considered people with the right "reach" who could help me open doors to accelerate or amplify my message.

But Jesus did something a little different, unexpected even. He assembled an eclectic group of men whose backgrounds didn't seem to align with His mission. Their qualifications weren't quite right. Considering this along with their innate flaws, tendencies, and character traits, most would say they weren't qualified to be on Jesus' short list. Here are the stories of some of the twelve:

- Simon Peter was a fisherman (Matthew 4:18). Peter was impulsive (Matthew 16:22–23) and sometimes lacked faith, as evidenced when he sank into the waves (Matthew 14:30–31). At the very end of Jesus' ministry, after three years of deep friendship and relationship, when the cock crowed, Peter denied knowing Jesus three times (Matthew 26:69–75).

- James and John were outspoken and were called the "sons of thunder" (Mark 3:17). In one instance, when a Samaritan village didn't welcome Jesus, the fiery James and John asked if they should call fire down from heaven and destroy it, prompting Jesus to rebuke them (Luke 9:51–54).
- Levi-Matthew was a tax collector, despised by all Jews (Matthew 9:9–10).
- Simon was a Zealot, part of an aggressive political movement that sought to incite rebellion against Rome (Matthew 10:4).
- Judas is known for being the treasurer (John 12:6) and for betraying Jesus, something Jesus must have known, but He still allowed him into His tribe.

I don't need to write any more to convince you the disciples were a messy bunch. But this imperfect group of men walked with Jesus and supported Him as He healed the sick, raised the dead, preached, taught, and lived out His purpose and life's mission to save the world for eternity.

I'm not suggesting you go out and find a tribe that doesn't align with your values. Nor am I suggesting you stay in unhealthy or abusive relationships. However, when we look at our tribes with new eyes, we may find that the tribes that change us and make us better aren't the easy tribes, but the messy ones. When we step back and consider the example of Christ, perhaps it's time to allow a little messiness in our lives.

Prayer

Dear God,

There are people in my life who are messy. There are days when they let me down. Give me wisdom and discernment to know who You would have in my life. Help me to look at my tribes with new eyes, to give each imperfect person a measure of grace as Your Son Jesus gave to those He walked with. Lord, no matter who You put in my life and on my path, help me to show them Your love. I know it won't always be easy, but with You I can do all things. In this moment, I praise You and thank You for my messy tribes. I also thank You for not giving up on me and for loving me as I bring my messiness to You.

Amen.

17

IF YOU DON'T KNOW ME BY NOW

KNOWING THEY'LL NEVER FULLY KNOW YOU, WHAT ACTIONS DO YOU NEED TO TAKE?

*"'...Who touched my clothes?'
'You see the people crowding against you,'
his disciples answered, 'and yet you can ask,
"Who touched me?"' But Jesus kept looking
around to see who had done it."*
—Mark 5:30–32 NIV

In my house, music and television are a big deal. Between my husband and my kids, there is guaranteed to be some audio-visual noisemaking device in almost every room. Personally, I prefer quiet music or perhaps a little television at low volume every now and again.

In addition to the volume levels, I live in a world of multiple device use. In my house, it would be common for me to come home and find a television blaring and a YouTube video running on the computer. Every now and then, someone might even be listening to something on their phone. Then, in the middle of all this chaos, someone attempts to have a conversation with me. I can't adequately explain what it feels like. As soon as they begin to speak, my brain starts to overload. I become overwhelmed with all the input. I want to run and hide.

I often think, *After all these years, don't they know me by now? Don't they know I can't handle all this noise?*

I'm sure my husband and kids think the opposite: *It isn't even that loud. Why is this such a big deal?*

While this may seem like a simple case of noise tolerance preferences, in my story, we find the root of another relationship challenge. What happens when that person—mother, father, husband, best friend, colleague, [fill in your blank]—in a relationship you have invested so much time in doesn't understand who you are?

Year after year, day after day, you've told them, shown them, and asked them, but they still don't seem to "get" you.

You just lost a loved one; shouldn't they know to come to the funeral to support you? You're struggling with an illness; shouldn't they know to drop some food off? You were rejected as a child; shouldn't they know you need to feel like you belong? Why can't they send an encouraging message if you're having a stressful time at work? You want to feel loved; shouldn't they know to hold you?

After all this time, shouldn't they know? What's the point of loving them as you do when, in the end, they just don't get you?

And that's when the stories begin.

Deep down in the recesses of our minds, we tell ourselves that maybe they don't love us or can't be trusted. We guard our hearts and watch their patterns. However, in some instances, watching the patterns doesn't help one bit. You see, when we watch someone's patterns through the lens of "I can't trust you," we'll always find exactly what we're looking for: their worst.

In Mark 5:30–32, we see one of those "why don't you know me" moments between Jesus and His disciples. He's walking through a large crowd, people clamoring to get to Him. Rocks jamming into their shoes, and bodies dripping with sweat as the crowd swells and presses harder and closer to Him with increasing urgency and need.

And then, in the middle of all that, Jesus asked, "Who touched me?"

The fact that His disciples heard Jesus is a testament that they loved Him and wanted to protect Him. They were close, surrounding Him and doing their best with their physical bodies to keep the people from crushing Him.

However, instead of asking, "What do you mean, Teacher?" they said (Leah's paraphrase), "Jesus! Can't you see we're doing our best to keep this crowd from crushing you to death? There are so many of them. Of course they're touching you. How can you ask, who touched me?"

At that moment, Jesus doesn't respond. He keeps looking around to see who touched Him. If you take a step back and think about it, this isn't the first time the disciples misunderstood or questioned Him, even though He was with them every day. With all that proximity, they still didn't understand who He was.

On a human level, you can imagine Jesus' frustration and disappointment:

"Why don't they understand?"

"Why don't they know my heart?"

"Why can't they see with new eyes?"

"Why don't they have more faith?"

Nestled in the pages of the Gospels and the life of Christ are two simple truths to help us respond to the age-old relationship question: Why don't you know me by now?

They'll Never Know

Jesus was perfect: perfectly fair, perfectly kind, and perfectly loving. Yet His disciples still didn't understand who He was. No matter how much you love people or how clear or vulnerable you are with them, they'll never truly know you. When you accept that, you can begin to tell yourself a different story. Instead of "they don't care," you can either let it go or ask, "What do I need to do to help them understand what I need?"

Think Different

Time and time again throughout His ministry, Jesus' disciples let Him down. But instead of cutting them off and casting them aside—instead of feeding Himself an internal story about how the disciples can't be trusted—Jesus does something else. He allows them to stay by His side and teaches what love is by modeling it through His actions every day. Then on the doorstep of his pending death, He gets down on His hands and knees and washes their feet.

When it comes to navigating relationships with the people we love, we should expect letdowns. However, our response to a letdown should never be to shut down. Instead of judging them through the lens of our pain, we can, as Jesus demonstrated, talk, set boundaries, give, and love.

It won't be easy. In fact, the only thing I can guarantee is that some days it will be hard. But our daily decisions to care, let go, or confront in love will help us navigate our relationships differently. When it comes to other people, they'll never really know you. But the beautiful thing is, when you choose to Think Different, they will always recognize the God in you.

Prayer

Dear Jesus,

I can't begin to tell You how many times I feel hurt and let down by those who are supposed to love me. In those moments when I feel so alone, help me. Be the comfort they cannot be. Instead of judging them, I want to share what I need in a way that strengthens our relationship. Thank You for setting an example for me to follow. Thank You for reminding me I can choose to think differently about people and situations. Thank You for being patient when I don't love You how I should. Finally, thank You for coming to earth to show me that when I choose to love like You, it can change everything.

Amen.

18

WHATEVER IT TAKES!

WHERE ARE YOU EXPERIENCING VALUES CONFLICT? WHAT DOES LOVE LOOK LIKE EVEN IN CONFLICT?

"...I have become all things to all people so that by all possible means I might save some. I do all this for the sake of the gospel, that I may share in its blessings."
—1 Corinthians 9:22–23 NIV

Many years ago, my brother stopped by my house. His company designed websites for clients. At that time, he was working with a client who developed family crests. The goal was to create something designed as a family heirloom to pass down from generation to generation. I remember thinking, *If I had one made, what would it say? What thoughts or sentiments would I want to pass down from generation to generation?*

Around the same time, I moved to a new company. As part of my onboarding, we spent a lot of time discussing values and principles.

The combination of these two experiences made me think, *If companies and leaders use values and beliefs to define behaviors they want to see, why don't more people have personal or family values?*

This thought initiated a seven-year process to define my core values. It was a deep exploration into what mattered most to me, and I took my time.

These days, in my coaching and programs, we define our values in less than seven years, of course! Values identification aims to serve as a foundation for determining how one wants to show up in their life and leadership. As believers, we have personal and spiritual values. But from time to time, something sinister happens. Without even realizing it, we allow our values to become a measuring stick we use to determine who we let in and move out of our lives. Values become beating sticks used to judge the actions of others.

When figuring out how to be values-led and heart-driven, it's worth considering Paul's strategy for connecting with people and winning them over. In 1 Corinthians 9:19–23, Paul said he willingly made himself a slave to everyone to win as many as possible. To the Jews, he became like a Jew. To those who didn't have the law, he became like someone who didn't have the law. To the weak, he became weak. He became all things to all people so they could be saved. Paul was intentionally flexible in his ministry to more easily connect with people and help them see who God is. His mindset was *whatever it takes.*

Values are important. They anchor us, but they also bring conflict. They help us to see when others' actions or beliefs don't align with our own. If we value integrity, we may struggle with the person who doesn't take care of their family and financial obligations. If we value excellence, we might be challenged by someone who throws things together. If we value kindness, we may struggle with someone who doesn't help during times of crisis.

I imagine at some point or another, you've been at odds with someone or even an organization based on your values. In these moments, the opportunity is to remember: Your values are yours. In fact, even if someone else had the exact same values, they probably wouldn't define them like you do. Values matter. They crystallize our beliefs, ground us, underpin our courage, and clarify when to act.

Today is a reminder to think differently. To not allow your values to become a harsh measuring stick or a hard beating stick. Your values are not the bar, but they can help you raise the bar. Like the Apostle Paul, perhaps your greatest opportunity is to be open to the moments where you might need to bend to share God's love. Your *whatever it takes* could be just the thing that changes everything.

Prayer

Dear God,

    Thank You for instilling values and beliefs to help anchor me to show up as the person You created me to be. Lord, forgive me for all the times I have used them to beat myself and others. Please help me think different. Instead of indifference, let me be curious. Instead of frustration, please help me see opportunities for change. Instead of judgment, give me *whatever-it-takes* boldness. Without a shadow of a doubt, I can't do it on my own, so I'm humbly asking for Your help.

Amen.

> **UNLOCK MORE:** Our values shape who we are and can sometimes cause friction when others don't share them. To help you embrace your unique values, I'm thrilled to offer you the Values Builder assessment. Discover how your values play a role in decisions and relationships, and use these insights to build stronger, more authentic connections. Head over to www.leahjmdean.com/bedifferenttribe to download your assessment and get started today.

19

NOT TODAY

WHAT OFFENSE MIGHT YOU NEED TO LET GO?

"A person's wisdom yields patience; it is to one's glory to overlook an offense."
—Proverbs 19:11 NIV

I live on the island of Bermuda, where it's customary to greet people with a "good morning" or "good afternoon." In the late 1990s, I moved to New York City. When I visited small shops or met people on the streets of Manhattan, my happy good mornings and hellos were often met with stares or stony silence. After a few years of rebuffs, I shifted from, "Good morning! How are you today?" to simply stating my request, "May I have a burrito with a side order of guacamole?"

One Christmas break, I traveled back to Bermuda. It was colder than usual, so I decided to pick up a pair of socks. I dropped into one of the local retail stores to find a pair that would suit my needs. I approached the cashier, who was casually talking to another worker.

I waited for a pause in their "non-work-related" conversation and said, "Excuse me, where can I find the socks?"

If you had been in the room, you would've felt the temperature drop as they looked at me silently. Unsure of what was happening, I repeated my request, "Excuse me, where can I find the socks?" They looked at me again, and there was another long, awkward pause.

Finally, seeing the puzzled look on my face, they said, "Good morning!!!"

My brain quickly clicked into "Bermuda mode," and I said, "I'm so sorry. Good morning. How are you today? Could you please tell me where the socks are?"

I've engaged in passionate debates about this scenario, which, back in those days, was often repeated across the island. Many other locals and guests alike have left similar interactions feeling very offended. As the customer, was it my responsibility to make the first gesture? Or was it the role of the customer service representative to greet me?

In the moment, I was offended, but I chose to adjust. It wasn't worth the fight. I just needed socks!

This is a simple example of how a minor interaction might offend. Here's another one: In my experience, more than ever before we use texting to communicate. Picking up the phone to talk when you're busy or on the run is becoming increasingly rare. Have you ever been offended by short, clipped text responses? Even worse, you can see the person has read your message but fails to respond for hours or even days.

I could go on and share scenario after scenario of offenses that happen every day, from the boss or colleague who speaks to you with the wrong tone to the child who ignores your request. Let's face it: We live in an offensive world!

I spoke to a large group of women while writing this book, and we discussed how sometimes it was difficult to overlook the many "micro-offenses" we encounter daily. We talked about the impact these offenses can have on our lives, and the health and psychological effects of holding on to them.

I love this devotional's text in the Amplified version: *"Good sense and discretion make a man slow to anger, and it is his honor and glory to overlook a transgression or an offense [without seeking revenge and harboring resentment]." (Proverbs 19:11 AMP)*

We can guarantee we'll be offended as we strive to live a life more reflective of Christ's character. The question then becomes, how can I challenge myself with "not today"?

The next time offense shows up at your doorstep, perhaps you can ask yourself, "Do I need to talk to this person who has a pattern of treating me this way?"

If the answer is "Yes," find the right time and space to talk about it. If the answer is "No," it might be an opportunity to choose, "Not today!"

I've found choosing *not today* to be liberating. Instead of allowing the offense to consume my thoughts for hours or sometimes days, I pray for control over my mind and decide to move on! This choice not only preserves my mental health but also fosters healthier relationships.

As you consider the relationships surrounding you, are you the offender or the offended? If you are the offender, how can you make amends? If you are the offended, and don't know what to do, get support to figure out your best next step. Whatever route you choose, the next time offense surfaces, and it surely will, perhaps your best option is to pause, breathe, pray, and say, "Not today!"

Prayer

Dear Father,

Often, I'm offended. In fact, my words, actions, and even my prayers may sometimes offend You! However, You are loving and patient when I fail repeatedly. When I'm the offender, please prompt me to apologize quickly so relationships can thrive and experience restoration. As I navigate home, work, and church, please help me to be patient and look for opportunities to forgive offenses as I decide not today. Please give me the wisdom to know when to address offense and when to move on. Thank You so much for Your patience with me and the work You are doing in me. I don't deserve it, but I'm very grateful. Thank You, thank You, thank You.

Amen.

20

WHAT ARE YOU TREASURING?

WHAT NEGATIVE THOUGHTS DO YOU NEED TO REPLACE WITH ACTION AND BOUNDARIES?

"For where your treasure is, there your heart will be also."
—Luke 12:34 NIV

We sat down for hours and talked. We mapped out precisely what we would do and how it would happen. We created a list and checked it twice. We had a plan. I had my part and they had theirs. The project end date was so close I could taste it! Only it didn't work out that way. I held up my part of the bargain, but theirs slipped through the cracks of life. It could have been a busy period, a catastrophe, or so many things. All I knew was that our carefully constructed plan fell apart, and I needed to pick up the pieces.

For weeks and then months this weighed on me. I picked up the pieces and got the task done. But inside, I was angry with them for letting us down, letting me down, or at least that is what I thought.

You see, anger is often a secondary emotion sitting atop a root emotion. When I stopped being angry, I realized what I was feeling was disappointment and hurt. Their lack of follow-through, without any heads-up or notice, even though it wasn't about me, translated to "You don't care."

There I was—stuck, hurt, and angry because things fell through, again.

Wait, again? What do you mean again? Immediately, my brain recalled all the times they said they would, and then they didn't. There was always a reason, sometimes a good reason, but the reality is, they just didn't.

I don't know about you, but I have found life is often full of "agains." Perhaps you expected they would never lie to you, but they did, again. You asked for feedback, but they clammed up, again. They said they would do it, but they forgot, again. You wanted them to care like you do, but they didn't, again. Perhaps you gave it 110 percent, but your 110 percent wasn't good enough, again.

Because "again" happens again and again; over time, our brain stores each experience. Though we want to let it go, every time *again* happens again, the past comes flooding to the surface.

This devotional's text is often used to talk about money and time. Where you invest your money and spend your time, that is where your heart is. One morning I woke up at 4:00 a.m., and as part of my morning devotion, I decided to look it up in the Greek. What I found was both affirming and surprising. In Greek, the word "treasure" in that text is *thésauros*, which means a storehouse of treasure, including (treasured) thoughts stored up in the heart and mind.[5]

At that moment, the Holy Spirit stopped me and said, "What thoughts about people and situations are you storing up in your mind? What hurts and disappointments are you holding on to?"

"But Lord, those aren't treasures; treasures are beautiful things, happy thoughts, and memories," I said.

He responded, "Treasures are anything you choose to keep and nurture. You wonder why that relationship won't change? Yet day after day, week after week, month after month, there are feelings and thoughts you're holding on to. You haven't talked it out. You haven't created boundaries. Yet here you are, storing up those thoughts and disappointments like treasures, and in the end, that leaves your mind tortured and you with a heart problem."

"Wow! Okay. I never thought about it like that!"

"What's the answer then?" God said.

"My child, the answer is to be more mindful of the thoughts you store in your mind about people and situations. If something is not sitting right with you, pray about it. Ask Me to give you clarity and show you if it's you. Sometimes, it's your behavior that needs to change. Sometimes, it's not you, but you need to create a boundary because the other person doesn't value what you value. At other times, you will need to have a conversation to release those thoughts, empty the storehouse of your mind, restore the relationship, and set your heart free!"

Pause for just a moment. Maybe you've been holding onto the memories and pain for way too long, and you feel tortured. Perhaps you've suppressed them, but they keep coming up again and again. This moment is a beautiful opportunity to start fresh. The Bible promises that where your treasure is, there your heart *will be* also. When you replace negative treasures with new treasures (thoughts and experiences) created through prayer, conversations, and boundaries, you *will* live free.

Prayer

> Dear Heavenly Father,
>
> It's time. I've been holding on to the pain for so long. I've thought about it, stewed over it, cried about it, pondered it, talked about it, and yet it's still there. God, I need to be free—free to love, free to forgive, free to move on. This morning, I ask for You to help me Think Different, release old treasures, and create new ones so I'm free to share who You are with others.
>
> Amen.

21

THE STORIES WE TELL OURSELVES

ARE THE STORIES YOU'VE TOLD YOURSELF INFLUENCING HOW YOU LOVE OTHERS?

"Which of these three do you think was a neighbor to the man who fell into the hands of robbers?"
—Luke 10:36 NIV

The other day, I was talking to a friend about why people are sometimes reluctant to build their tribes. We concluded sometimes we're unwilling to be open because we've told ourselves a story about the other person.

Our past hurts and experiences lead us to fabricate tales, often without conversations or facts. Sometimes, without even realizing it, we put unsuspecting people and potential relationships into boxes. I remember one occasion when I did just that. There was a woman on the outskirts of my professional circle who was a bit "aloof."

Whenever I saw or thought about her, an unease would settle in, and I would tell myself a story. One night, I was at an event when who should I see walking through the crowd coming toward me? This same woman.

I need to pause here because we sometimes allow the stories we've created to shape our interactions. I saw the woman coming and I had three options:

1. Move away to ensure she didn't see me
2. Engage with someone else so I was unavailable as she walked by
3. Say hello

I chose option three: be open and say hello.

The woman walked straight toward me. We locked eyes. She broke out into a big smile as she approached me. She immediately started to share how much she was encouraged by my work and looked forward to my messages and newsletters.

As I wrote this devotional, I wanted to delete this story. Until now, I have not shared it. So, why be vulnerable and share it with you now? Because the reality is, I'm not alone. Every day, we create stories in our thought life. Whether we like it or not, those stories shape our relationships. The crazy thing is, in many instances, the people we're thinking about have so much going on in their lives they're not even thinking about us!

I believe God allowed me to have this chance interaction with her so I could share it with you. A reminder to us all: Until you know, you *don't* know. Here's the thing: Sometimes the thoughts we have are God-given discernment and wisdom. However, even if we *do* know as believers, we should never allow the stories to impact how we treat others.

To help us out, Jesus gave us clear instructions in Matthew 5:43–48: love our enemies and pray for those who persecute us. That means, whether we're dealing with an actual enemy or an enemy created because of the stories in our heads, our response should always be the same: *love*.

A great example of this in the Bible is found in Luke 10:30–36 in the parable of the Good Samaritan. A Jewish man was beaten, wounded by thieves, and left for dead. While he was lying on the side of the road fighting for his life, a priest and then a Levite passed by and ignored him. However, when the Samaritan man saw him, he immediately sprang into action and met his needs. This was a *big* deal!

To understand the animosity between the Jews and the Samaritans, we need a little of the backstory. Samaritans were Jews in part of the northern kingdom of Israel. They were a nation that refused to be ruled by the descendants of David (1 Kings 12:19), they worshiped idols (1 Kings 12:28–33), and they intermarried with the Assyrians (Ezra 9:1–10). Many Jews considered them half-breeds or dogs, and there was an ongoing rift between the two groups.

Now take a step back. Because of the history between the Jews and the Samaritans, the Samaritan probably had some concrete examples of personal or generational discrimination that could've led him to pass the injured man by. Instead, he had compassion. He took care of the injured man's wounds and paid for him to be cared for. At the end of the parable, Jesus instructed his listeners to be like the Good Samaritan.

My hope and prayer for you is that you can put aside, or at least reconsider, the stories you tell yourself. Then ask yourself, how can I be a good neighbor?

The reality is we won't know until we know, and even when we do, our mission remains the same: move in and love.

Prayer

Dear God,

I'm asking for Your help. Some days it's difficult to turn off the stories I tell myself and the scars of past hurts and experiences. Lord, help me to think differently and show up like the Good Samaritan, with compassion and love. It's easier said than done, so thank You in advance for Your help.

Amen.

22

CAPTIVE THOUGHTS

WHAT THOUGHTS ABOUT SITUATIONS AND PEOPLE CAN YOU GIVE TO GOD?

"We are destroying sophisticated arguments and every exalted and proud thing that sets itself up against the [true] knowledge of God, and we are taking every thought and purpose captive to the obedience of Christ."
—2 Corinthians 10:5 AMP

I don't know about you, but to my dismay, I have opinions about everything! No matter how hard I try, I still have a view. It's bothered me for years because opinions feel like the spirit of judgment. And doesn't Matthew 7:1–3 remind us never to judge and that the speck we see in someone else's eye is not as bad as the plank in our own eye? I try to "Think Different" and stay neutral. But no matter how hard I try, I still have opinions!

One of the services I offer my clients is strengths-based assessments and coaching. I love strengths work because the idea that God created natural talents that can be cultivated into strengths is powerful. Studying my strengths taught me I'm a maximizer, wired to be a catalyst for change. Like a diver after pearls, I search out ways to help make people and situations better, which means, like it or not, I'm going to have opinions.

While writing this book, I began a season of searching. A season of asking God to change our relationship, to ensure that however and wherever I spent my time was aligned with His assignment for my life. Around that same time, a spiritual mentor and friend invited me to fast with her.

On this particular day of fasting, as I was praying, I asked God to reveal to me one of the areas I needed to focus on. During the fast I felt impressed to repent against the spirit of judgment. But first I wanted to understand what repentance really meant.

In Luke 5:32 NIV, Jesus said, *"I have not come to call the righteous, but sinners to repentance."* In Greek, the word for repentance is *metanoia*, which means a change of mind.[6] *Metanoia* comes from the word *metanoeó*, which comes from *metá* (*"changed after* being *with"*) and *noéō* ("think").[7] In essence, Jesus was saying, "I came to help sinners Think Different after being with Me."

I hope you're getting excited. You see, your original thought or opinion is not the sin. Through this text God is saying to you, "I wired you to think. However, when you give those thoughts to me, I can change you. I can help you Think Different. I can help you take those negative thoughts captive and turn them into actions that benefit others and build up My kingdom."

As I got up from my chair that day, for the first time in a long time, I felt free. Free to be me, with all my thoughts and opinions, and clear about where to go when they started to turn negative or feel too heavy.

As we wrap up this pillar on thinking differently, I want you to know that this same freedom is yours. Your thoughts don't have to be a sin, but merely a moment in time. At any time you can ask God to help you take your negative thoughts about people or situations captive. At any moment you can ask for wisdom about how to respond. What thoughts can you give to Him today?

Prayer

My patient Heavenly Father,

The struggle is real. It's a battle to escape what I think about people and situations and find lasting peace. God, I acknowledge the desire inside of me to judge. I ask for forgiveness and help. Change me. Please help me to prioritize spending time with You so You can take my thoughts captive. From this moment forward, please help me turn my thoughts into words and actions that allow others to see You in me.

Amen.

Reflect & Renew

Relationships will always challenge us. What we want or expect and what people actually do will often be miles apart. As we wrap up this third pillar—Think Different—take a few moments to reflect on the questions we've explored in our journey so far. Ask God to show you where He wants you to grow.

LISTEN DIFFERENT

1. Is it time to pause and listen for God's direction in your busy life?
2. How can you be more intentional about finding or creating space to pause?
3. Have you asked God to help you live out His plan for your life? If not, why?
4. What tribes do you have or need to build?

TRUST DIFFERENT

5. In what ways can you lean on God to help you fight and win your battles?
6. How might adopting the way God sees you impact your life?
7. What steps could you take to believe in your value even when you're not doing something big?

⑧ How might believing that God is in your tribe transform your confidence?

⑨ What voices do you need to quiet? What past victories can you remember?

⑩ In what ways has God used your past pain as preparation?

⑪ What steps do you need to take to stop comparing yourself to others?

⑫ How can you move forward using the strengths and gifts you have?

⑬ Where might God be calling you to influence change?

THINK DIFFERENT

⑭ How can you choose love and practice peace daily?

⑮ What thoughts or feelings about people might you need to let go?

⑯ What messiness in your tribe might you need to let in?

⑰ Knowing they'll never fully know you, what actions do you need to take?

⑱ Where are you experiencing values conflict? What does love look like even in conflict?

⑲ What offense might you need to let go?

⑳ What negative thoughts do you need to replace with action and boundaries?

㉑ Are the stories you've told yourself influencing how you love others?

㉒ What thoughts about situations and people can you give to God?

talk DIFFERENT

PILLAR FOUR

Talk Different

I'm so excited to share this next part of the journey with you. As an advisor and coach, I spend a considerable amount of my time helping people prepare for conversations. Difficult conversations, courageous conversations, risky conversations—I like to think of them as *Necessary Conversations*™. Whatever you call them, the way we speak to each other has the power to change lives. As you turn the page to Pillar Four, Talk Different, I invite you to explore the practical lessons, tips, and tools we can use to show up differently with our words. It won't be easy, but it will always be worth it.

Words create and destroy. Speak life!

23

BUT WHY DID YOU NEED TO SEARCH?

IN WHAT RELATIONSHIPS DO YOU
NEED TO BE MORE DIRECT
BUT NOT DEFENSIVE?

*"'But why did you need to search?' he asked.
'Didn't you know that I must be
in my Father's house?'"*
—Luke 2:49 NLT

When living and thriving with our tribes, one of the most important contributors to the success of our relationships is how we speak to each other. In fact, while writing this chapter, I spoke to someone who was angry and hurt because a colleague had spoken to them so disrespectfully. It was painful to listen as they recounted their experience. The conversation reminded me that how we speak to each other in our relationships will either paralyze us, keep us stuck, or keep us moving forward. Let's dig in.

Our first conversation in this pillar takes place in Luke Chapter 2. Jesus and His family traveled to Jerusalem to celebrate Passover. The Passover was a time of remembrance of the last night of bondage in Egypt. On that first Passover night, at midnight, the angel of the Lord struck down all of the firstborns in Egypt, including firstborn livestock! However, if the children of Israel obeyed and sprinkled the doorpost with blood as God commanded, the lives of their firstborn children were spared.

At the end of the annual Passover feast in Jerusalem, Mary and Joseph left with the caravan, believing Jesus was somewhere in the group. But after traveling for a day, they searched for Him among relatives and acquaintances. When they couldn't find Him, they were beside themselves and rushed back to Jerusalem to search for Him.

As a parent, I can imagine their horror. When my son was about nine or ten years old, we traveled to Boston. At some hour in the morning, I was yanked from my sleep by the phone.

"Good morning. Is this Mrs. Dean?"

"Yes," I answered, my brain barely awake.

"We have your son here at the front desk. A guest found him wandering through the halls. Would you like me to have someone bring him back to your room?"

"Yes, please," I replied as I hung up the phone.

As soon as the phone handle's weight hit the cradle, my brain woke up. *Wait! What! My son is not next to me in the next bed! Why was he wandering around the halls?* I thought to myself as I woke up my husband.

I can't describe the sheer panic I felt as my brain processed everything that could have gone wrong. Those five minutes we waited for the knock on the door for my son's return felt like five hours.

If my experience was for five minutes, just imagine what it must've felt like for Jesus' parents. Three whole long, anxious, panic-filled days, searching for Jesus! I imagine the additional weight of who Jesus was and the purpose of His life probably added a layer of stress for Mary and Joseph.

On the third day, they finally found Jesus. He was in the temple.

When His mother saw Him, she said, *"Son, why have you done this to us? Your Father and I have been frantic, searching for you everywhere."* Jesus, at the age of twelve, looks at His parents and says, *"'But why did you need to search?... Didn't you know that I must be in my Father's house?'" (Luke 2:48–49 NLT)*

When I project my emotions into that discussion, I would've been somewhere between wanting to hug and strangle my son. I also know I would've been annoyed if my son had said to me after three days of sheer panic, "Why were you looking for me?"

When it comes to communication, what can we learn from this mother-and-son conversation?

Speak clearly. Jesus' conversation with His mom demonstrates you can be direct without being disrespectful.

We see the heart and character of Jesus play out in the final verses of Luke 2:51–52. The Bible says He went down to Nazareth with His parents and was submissive and obedient to them. His mother treasured all these things in her heart. It also says He increased in wisdom and found favor with God and men. Jesus' pattern, as evidenced through His life and ministry, was perfectly respectful and perfectly loving. This is a gentle reminder: One-off conversations can't dictate the heart of a person with 100 percent precision. It's the patterns of how they show up that tell us who they really are.

The next time you're in a conversation with the potential to go off the rails, remember twelve-year-old clear, calm, and direct Jesus. Never forget to check the patterns of communication of yourself and the other party. A one-off challenging conversation never has to dictate who we are or our relationships for years to come.

Prayer

> Dear Heavenly Father,
> You know I struggle when people speak to me disrespectfully, and sometimes I can be a bit short. I struggle with this everywhere: at home, at work, and even with my fellow believers. Please transform how I speak to others.

Please help me be direct but not defensive. Clear but not condescending. Please help me be more like Jesus, and grow me in ways to impact people for Your kingdom. Thank You in advance for what only You can do.

    Amen.

24

THE POWER IN THE PAUSE

WHAT STRATEGIES COULD HELP YOU TO PAUSE BEFORE RESPONDING?

"Understand this, my dear brothers and sisters: You must all be quick to listen, slow to speak, and slow to get angry."
—James 1:19 NLT

One day, as I was driving to an appointment, the radio show hosts were talking about a politician caught on a hot mic. Instead of checking the mic before he spoke, the politician allowed his emotions to get the best of him and blurted out words he would soon live to regret. Those words said in a moment of passion and anger are now plastered in news reports, articles, and YouTube videos.

When I coach leaders about relationship dynamics, we often talk about the power of the pause. In our daily lives, sometimes we're confronted with situations we didn't see coming. We're often unprepared for these moments, and our first instinct is to lash out or give the person a piece of our mind.

The words in James 1:19 remind us to take a moment before we speak. Sometimes it might appear that someone is being disrespectful. But when we pause, we're often given a front-row seat to the authentic reality of the situation, like the angry spouse marginalized at work or the child who is battling doubt or depression. Or maybe it's the boss who's distracted because their spouse has cancer. When we pause between the triggering moment and our response, we create the capacity to calm emotions and consider alternatives.

Throughout the Bible, we see God pause. The story of Sodom and Gomorrah is a master class on responding to situations that might deserve a harsh response. When the story begins, instead of wiping the people of Sodom and Gomorrah off the face of the earth, God paused and decided to talk to Abraham.

God said, *"…I have heard a great outcry from Sodom and Gomorrah, because their sin is so flagrant. I am going down to see if their actions are as wicked as I have heard. If not, I want to know." (Genesis 18:20–21 NLT)*

Think about that. God knew the wickedness of Sodom and had a plan for destruction but chose to pause and go deeper first. When it comes to managing conversations and situations, we may think we know what's going on, but unlike God, we don't know everything.

What's interesting about this story is even though God already knew the answers, God invites Abraham into His deliberations. The lesson for us is, even if you have a plan or think you know the correct answer, it's always an excellent choice to stop, observe, and hunt for facts.

Not only does God invite Abraham into His planning, but He also allows Abraham to negotiate outcomes. Abraham asks God, *"Suppose you find 50 righteous people living there in the city—will you still sweep it away and not spare it for their sakes?"* God agrees. (Genesis 18:24 NLT)

Abraham then asks five more times: What if there are forty-five, forty, thirty, twenty, and finally ten righteous people? And God agrees that if there are ten righteous people, He will not destroy Sodom.

This story also demonstrates that we achieve better outcomes when we listen.

God could have destroyed Sodom and Gomorrah without engaging Abraham, but instead, He listened. As a result, Abraham knew no matter the outcome, God cared, and the decision was just and fair. When we invite others in, we open the door for acceptance because we've listened and considered.

I'm sure you can imagine a situation—or two or three or more—where God's been slow to anger and patient with you. Perhaps the next time you're tempted to react to someone else, you can respond with a peaceful pause. As we learned through the story of Abraham, tapping into the power of the pause can lead to answers, new perspectives, and better outcomes.

Prayer

Dear Father,

    I try to hold my tongue, but often the words slip out. When this happens, I don't experience outcomes that honor You, work for me, or work for anyone else. Help me to be more like You: wise, long-suffering, and patient. Please help me pause the words I speak and actions I take to honor You. I know I can't do this consistently on my own, so my request is simple: God, please give me the power to pause. Thank You so much for doing what only You can do.

    Amen.

25

AVOID AVOIDING CONFLICT

IN WHAT RELATIONSHIPS MIGHT YOU NEED TO STOP AVOIDING CONFLICT?

"Now Adonijah, whose mother was Haggith, put himself forward and said, 'I will be king.' So he got chariots and horses ready, with 50 men to run ahead of him. His father had never rebuked him by asking, 'Why do you behave as you do?...'"
—1 King 1:5–6 NIV

Have you ever been quiet when you should've said something because you didn't want to hurt someone's feelings? Or perhaps you're angry and felt it best to remain silent? Maybe you're so triggered you couldn't form the right words. You decided instead to wait for the right time, only the right time never came. Has this ever been you?

In my work, almost every client wants to talk about conflict and having "difficult conversations." No matter who we are, conversations consume us in ways we underestimate. You see, words are powerful. They control us, torture us, push us. Words can also set us free. Many of us can give great advice, but when conflict is personal, sometimes the words won't come, and time slips by.

We see a messy example of conflict avoidance in 1 Kings 1 when David's son Adonijah sets himself up as king. Now David is so old and fragile that he needs a female "bed warmer" just to help him keep the chill off his body. While David is in this delicate state, Adonijah proceeds to go out and secure chariots, horses, and fifty men to ride ahead of him as he prepares to appoint himself king. No asking. No permission. He just decided on his own to be king.

As I read, I thought, *What happened in their relationship to cause Adonijah to treat his father with such disrespect?* In the middle of the story, we get a window into their relationship and why this might've happened. The Bible says his father had never rebuked him by asking, "*Why do you behave as you do?...*" *(1 King 1:6 NIV)*

In this one sentence, we begin to see clearly this was not a one-off incident, but a pattern of conversation and conflict avoidance cultivated over time. This wasn't the first time Adonijah decided he wanted to do something and just did it. Over the years, David had allowed this behavior to blossom into brazen disregard and indifference.

When we avoid conflict, we sign up to deal with behaviors likely to frustrate us and potentially hurt others. We also embolden and inspire the other party to repeat the behavior again and again.

In my first book, *Assemble the Tribe*, I wrote about an exchange I had with a friend who was putting off a conversation in the name of peace.[8] I asked her, "Are you protecting the peace or perpetuating the problem?"

In this story of David and Adonijah, we see a grave example of what happens when we spend year after year protecting the peace. Right now, you might be thinking, *Oh dear, this is so me!* The good news is there are a few simple strategies you can use to tackle conflict head-on.

Pray

Often, when our emotions are high, we overreact. Take time to ask God to clarify the situation so you can approach it calmly. The Bible clarifies why taking this time to calm down is important. *"Fools give full vent to their rage, but the wise bring calm in the end." (Proverbs 29:11 NIV)* You will need God's help to figure out the right approach and the right timing. Just because you're ready doesn't mean they are.

Prepare

When you need to have a conversation, prepare your mind. Ask God for wisdom on timing, and don't put it off. Conversations delayed are conversations eventually replayed. If you need help preparing, get support from a trusted friend, coach, or counselor.

Talk in Private

Sometimes you might be tempted to confront someone in public. This could result in an embarrassing moment for them and you. In Matthew 18:15, Jesus encourages us to speak to those who offend us in private. Find a quiet place and pull them aside.

Don't Stack the Conversation

As we discussed in the last chapter, when someone hurts us, our emotions are triggered. All of their frustrating actions and behaviors come bubbling to the surface like a volcano about to erupt. In these moments, resisting the urge to tackle all the issues is essential. Instead, focus on the situation at hand, deal with that one topic, and stay there. A good rule to live by—one conversation, one topic.

Speak the Truth in Love

When dealing with conflict, imagine how you would approach it if you loved that person more than anyone else in the world. When I ask myself, "What words would I use if I truly loved this person?" I find the words flow much easier. The next time you need to deal with a difficult situation, give it a try.

Be Consistent

Behavioral change is never a one-off thing. The real work is being consistent with your communication. Spend some time thinking and praying about how you'll need to act and talk differently so you can change the pattern over time.

If you find yourself struggling with conflict avoidance, it's important not to be too hard on yourself. Ask God to reveal to you all the situations where you might be avoiding conflict. Then, ask God to give you the strength to avoid avoiding conflict so you can have healthier, happier, and more peaceful tomorrows.

Prayer

Dear Heavenly Father,

    I thought I was on top of it, but I avoid conflict. In this moment, I can hear You speaking to me. I can see the patterns of tomorrow I'm creating because I'm avoiding the conflict. God, it's not easy. Please give me the right words to deal with the conflict quickly, effectively, and in love. Lord, forgive me for all the times I've avoided the conflict. Please help me to unravel what I have failed to do in the past. Thank You for the wisdom, words, and will to be the change You created me to be.

    Amen.

26

FRUIT-LACED PARABLES

HOW CAN FOLLOWING JESUS' EXAMPLE TRANSFORM YOUR COMMUNICATION WITH OTHERS?

"A tree is identified by its fruit. If a tree is good, its fruit will be good. If a tree is bad, its fruit will be bad. And I tell you this, you must give an account on judgment day for every idle word you speak. The words you say will either acquit you or condemn you."
—Matthew 12:33 & 36–37 NLT

I was sitting in my kitchen one evening when I received a call from a friend who recently called *her* friend—let's call her Jaz—asking for prayer. Instead of praying, Jaz talked about a few messages she felt "led" to share. Her words were hurtful. My friend was left stunned. She struggled to understand why Jaz's "messages" were so harsh.

As I processed what my friend was saying, I was annoyed and hurt along with her. How could someone who was supposed to be a friend be so insensitive?

To my friend's credit, she didn't tell me the person's name or tear her down. All she did was ask, again and again, "How could she be so hurtful?" Later that evening, I decided to research how Jesus spoke to others during His time on Earth. Let's explore together.

In Matthew Chapter 10, Jesus is talking with the Pharisees about healing a man with a deformed hand. The Pharisees asked Jesus, *"'Does the law permit a person to work by healing on the Sabbath?' (They were hoping he would say yes, so they could bring charges against him.) And He answered, 'If you had a sheep that fell into a well on the Sabbath, wouldn't you work to pull it out? Of course you would. And how much more valuable is a person than a sheep! Yes, the law permits a person to do good on the Sabbath.'"* (Matthew 12:10–12 NLT) Jesus then reached out to the man and healed him. The Pharisees were so angry they began to plot to kill Him.

Fast-forward to Matthew 13, when Jesus shares several parables with His disciples. At the beginning of the chapter, His disciples asked Him, *"'…Why do you use parables when you talk to the people?' Jesus replied, '…to those who listen to my teaching, more understanding will be given, and they will have an abundance of knowledge. But for those who are not listening, even what little understanding they have will be taken away from them.'"* (Matthew 13:10–12 NLT)

In John Chapter 10, Jesus has another encounter and exchange.

> *It was now winter, and Jesus was in Jerusalem at the time of Hanukkah, the Festival of Dedication. He was in the Temple, walking through the section known as Solomon's Colonnade. The people surrounded him and asked, "How long are you going to keep us in suspense? If you are the Messiah, tell us plainly." Jesus replied, "I have already told you, and you don't believe me. The proof is the work I do in my Father's name. But you don't believe me because you are not my sheep. My sheep listen to my voice; I know them, and they follow me." (John 10:22–27 NLT)*

As I sat with these exchanges Jesus had with the Pharisees and His disciples, it was easy to see that Jesus was a very capable communicator. However, if you study His ministry, you'll find there are differences in the way He spoke. When interacting with the poor, oppressed, sick, and hurting people or those who wanted to hear His teachings, He spoke in stories they could understand, and His words were clear and kind. With the Pharisees who had hardened their hearts to His ministry, sometimes He was more direct.

In Matthew 12:33 & 36–37, Jesus reminded us that a tree is identified by its fruit. If a tree is good, its fruit will be good. If a tree is bad, its fruit will be bad. We know from Galatians 5:22–23 that the fruits of the Spirit are love, joy, peace, patience, kindness, goodness, faithfulness, gentleness, and self-control. When we feel led to share our opinions or give advice, we can ask ourselves: Are the words I'm about to say laced with fruit?

God desires for His people to grow closer to Him and show others who He is. The Bible says, *"Therefore if any man be in Christ, he is a new creature: old things are passed away; behold, all things are become new." (2 Corinthians 5:17 KJV)*

In the end, do I know if Jaz, the woman my friend called, was sincere in her words? I have an opinion, but I really don't know. What I do know is our choice of words reveals the condition of our hearts and will either create connections or build walls. The exciting news is that when we invite Jesus into our hearts, the words we choose to speak will be lined and oozing with good fruit. I want to claim that promise, don't you?

Prayer

Dear Heavenly Father,

Thank You for being so patient with me. I ask for forgiveness for all the times I have judged or spoken about someone with idle words. Thank You for reminding me to be thoughtful about my conversations and that my words should always be mixed with a healthy dose of fruit. I know I will only consistently say the right things if Your Spirit lives in me. Please help me speak life into people and situations and ooze fruit. Thank You.

Amen.

27

SPEAK SOFTLY AND CARRY A BEAGLE

HOW IS THE TONE OF YOUR VOICE IMPACTING YOUR COMMUNICATIONS?

"A gentle answer turns away wrath, but a harsh word stirs up anger."
—Proverbs 15:1 NIV

The other day, I was talking to a friend about a project she was working on with a colleague. Based on her colorful commentary, I would describe the individual she spoke about as a bull in a china shop. Have you ever met a person like that? The person who will speak their mind and say whatever they want?

In frustration, my friend said, "I'm a people person. I believe we shouldn't speak to people any old way! I think I'm going to just leave the organization!"

Growing up, my brother loved to watch Charlie Brown. Even to this day, I remember one episode in which Sally, Charlie Brown's little sister, complained to Charlie Brown about how the kids at the playground were bullying her. In frustration, she decides to take matters into her own hands and says to Charlie Brown, "I'm not out to start any trouble, but I'm also not afraid of them. I'm taking the advice of Theodore Roosevelt—speak softly and carry a beagle." She then picks up Snoopy, the family dog, and marches around the playground. Whenever a bully confronts her, she tells them she deserves to be there. Then, on command, Snoopy barks and growls until the bully runs away.

Sometimes, we can be like Sally. The way people act and speak frustrates us so much it stirs up anger to the point we feel we have no choice but to "fight back." At our wits' end, we find ourselves looking for ways to "put the bull in the china shop" in their place.

In the case of Sally, the "fight back" method is so effective that she begins to change. What started as a means to protect herself begins to alter who she is. In the last scene, we see her bullying a kid, telling them the beagle will bite them if they don't move out of her way. The kid then says, "What beagle?" Sally turns around to find Snoopy has left her, and her words don't have any bite at all.

The Bible text for this devotional reading reminds us of the power of our words. They can bring calm or stir things up! In their book *Words Can Change Your Brain*, Mark Waldman and Andrew Newberg write that just saying the word "No" activates the production of cortisol, the stress hormone.[9] Conversely, dopamine, a hormone that regulates gratification, is triggered when we say "Yes." Imagine the effects of the wrong words and a harsh tone.

When we get comfortable speaking to people any old way, the repercussions can have deep tentacles. Not only will others want to distance themselves from us, but we may lay seeds of hurt and hate with consequences more profound than we ever intended. Those seeds of harsh words stir up pain and cause people to leave organizations, churches, and even families. In the end, no one wins.

No matter the day, the words we say and how we say them matter. Chapter 26 was about our choice of words, and this devotional offers an opportunity to reflect on the tone of our words. You've probably heard the adage "It's not what you say but how you say it." If we want to heal and help our relationships, we can ask ourselves, "When I speak, am I using a tone that evokes stress or anger?" Maybe your greatest opportunity for impact is to speak softly and leave the beagle at home.

Prayer

Dear Father,
 Every day I speak, but some days I fail to speak with a tone that helps others experience You. Lord, I don't want my words to stir up seeds of hurt or hate. Please help me to speak with a gentle firmness that helps heal relationships and build bridges. I know I can't do it on my own.

Thank You for Your loving patience, which paved the way for me to change. Finally, God, where I have planted seeds of harshness, please soothe the hearts of those I may have hurt and show me where to make amends.

    Amen.

28

DON'T SINK MY BOAT

**DO YOU HAVE A TRIBE THAT
OFFERS WISE, GODLY COUNSEL?
IF NOT, WHO MIGHT YOU REACH OUT TO?**

*"The sailors were terrified when
they heard this, for he had already told
them he was running away from the Lord.
'Oh, why did you do it?' they groaned."*
—Jonah 1:10 NLT

When my son was in grade school, he was very relaxed. Very rarely did he get in trouble. When he did, it was for being more interested in his thoughts than whatever was happening in the classroom! On rare occasions, he would come home upset. When I asked him what was wrong, he'd say, "I got in trouble!"

"What happened?" I'd ask.

"Some of the kids were talking while the teacher was teaching, and the whole class got into trouble, and I had to stay in during recess!"

Oh, the age-old innocent suffering for the guilty complaint! The book of Jonah tells another story about the innocent suffering for the guilty.

Often when we read the book of Jonah, we get swept away by the swallowed-by-the-whale part of the story. But one day, I found myself drawn to the pages of Jonah in a different way. I wanted to read about this prophet who was called by God, given clear instructions, and, instead of obeying, ran away.

In Jonah 1:1–2, God tells Jonah to go to Nineveh and warn the people to change their ways. By verse 3, Jonah has gone to Joppa, purchased a ticket, and booked a trip in the opposite direction. I find this a little bizarre. Jonah was a prophet, so we can assume he had an intimate relationship with God. Jonah also knew that God is everywhere. So it boggles my mind that Jonah thought he could run away. As the boat leaves for Tarshish, Jonah decides to take a nap. Meanwhile, God unleashes a powerful storm that threatens to break the ship apart.

The sailors cry out to their gods without success. After some time, the captain goes to find Jonah, wakes him up, and shouts,

> "How can you sleep at a time like this? Get up and pray to your god! Maybe he will pay attention to us and spare our lives." Then, the crew cast lots to see who had offended the gods and caused the terrible storm. When they did this, the lots identified Jonah as the culprit. "Why has this awful storm come down on us?" they demanded. "Who are you? What is your line of work? What country are you from? What is your nationality?"

Jonah answers,

> "I am a Hebrew, and I worship the Lord, the God of heaven, who made the sea and the land." The sailors were terrified when they heard this, for he had already told them he was running away from the Lord. "Oh, why did you do it?" they groaned. (Jonah 1:6–10 NLT)

Let's pause and park at this point in the story. What struck me as I read these verses is that because Jonah chose to operate outside God's will, he endangered the lives of those around him. An example of the innocent suffering for the guilty. If you think about it, we do the same thing every day with our words.

We're frustrated by people and situations, so we find a group, friend, or even strangers to share exactly what is on our minds. Don't get me wrong—sometimes we need a place to talk and make sense of our feelings. However, there is a difference between "I'm struggling with this and need support to process and pray" and gossiping about people and situations. Let's get a little more specific.

Have you ever had a conversation with someone, and the conversation is moving along, and then someone shares an opinion, tidbit, or juicy piece of gossip that changes the entire tone or nature of the conversation? You were "sailing along in your boat of life," then, like Jonah, their gossip or negative words brought the storm.

Just like God's explicit instruction to Jonah, the Bible provides specific instruction when it comes to how we should talk about people and situations: *"Do not let any unwholesome talk come out of your mouths, but only what is helpful for building others up according* to their needs, that it may benefit those who listen." (Ephesians 4:29 NIV)

Just like the sailors who had to live through Jonah's storm, when we inject negativity into our conversations, we bring storms into the lives of others. Not only does our negativity bring frustration in the moment, but sometimes the words we share alter thoughts, opinions, and relationships for years to come.

If I make this personal, sometimes I need to get things off my chest. But the more I learn about the importance of speaking life into situations, the more I feel led to talk to God about it. Instead of sharing my frustrations with just anyone, I try to limit my conversations to a spiritual mentor or individual who will encourage me with a Godly perspective. More and more, I'm convinced that before we share, there are a few powerful questions we can ask ourselves:

1. Have I prayed about it?
2. Why am I about to share this?
3. Is this the right person to talk to about this?
4. How will my words impact the listener?
5. Should I hold my tongue?

During World War II, the phrase "Loose lips sink ships" began appearing on US posters. The poster design was intended to remind and encourage people not to carelessly talk and share information that might undermine the war effort. The British used the phrase "Careless talk costs lives." The Swedish promoted "A Swede keeps silent," and the Germans used "Shame on you, blabbermouth!"[10] While some historians argue that the primary goal of these phrases was to censor the people, the fact remains that in times of war, if someone said the wrong thing to the wrong person, lives were lost.

For the past two chapters, we have discussed choice and tone of words. In this chapter, as we reflect on the timing and recipients of our words, we are reminded that at any moment, we can bring peace or pain into the lives of those around us. Like David, we can pray, *"Let the words of my mouth, and the meditation of my heart, be acceptable in thy sight, O Lord, my strength, and my redeemer." (Psalm 19:14 KJV)* I believe that with God's help, our words will lift people and situations up and never sink someone else's boat.

Prayer

Dear Heavenly Father,

    I'm human, and sometimes I need a release. I need a place to feel hurt, disappointed, and frustrated. In those moments, please help me to choose You first. Please help me remember You can comfort me in ways no human can! And when I need human advisors, Lord, help me to be wise and discerning and not vent with just anyone at any time. Instead, help me connect with people who can support me, pray with me, and remind me who You have called me to be. Thank You for being so patient and thank You for Your love.

    Amen.

29

HEAL THE SCAB

DO YOU EXPERIENCE OFFENSE IN YOUR RELATIONSHIPS?

"An offended friend is harder to win back than a fortified city. Arguments separate friends like a gate locked with bars."
—Proverbs 18:19 NLT

I was preparing dinner for my daughter. I popped a bowl of soup in the microwave. When the alarm went off to signal it was complete, in a hurry I grabbed it with my hands instead of using the pot holders. As I picked up the piping-hot bowl of soup, I stumbled. The scalding soup splashed everywhere, including on my wrist! Within seconds, I could see a quarter-sized burn developing. The pain was excruciating, and I was annoyed with myself for being so careless. I quickly put some cold water on it and ran to the cabinet for ointment.

For the next few weeks, I was determined to help heal the burn as quickly as possible. I put ointment on it daily, and it started to scab over. But every night, when I ran it under water, the scab came off, slowing down the healing process and reminding me of my careless mistake.

While I was still nursing my burn back to health, I had a conversation with a friend, and we concluded that sometimes our relationships are like scabs. There's this "thing" the other person does that opens a wound or frustrates and unsettles you over and over. It could be that the relationship is suffering from offense, which we talked about in Chapter 19.

In this reading, let's focus on what we do when the repeat offender pushes us to the point that we lose our cool and speak words we can't ever take back.

According to the Merriam–Webster dictionary, an offense outrages the moral or physical senses.[11] Here are two examples I've coached people through:

Perhaps someone says something that pulls you down or lets you down. In the moment, you let it roll off your back and say nothing. However, when you say nothing, over time their behavior becomes more frequent and bolder. The scab of offense is reopened again and again!

Or consider this: Perhaps the offense isn't coming from someone else, but it's coming from you! Without even realizing it, you offend the other person over and over.

Does any of this sound familiar?

Are there individuals in your life who routinely offend you? Maybe you're aware of the offense. Or maybe you didn't realize until this very moment that the feeling that you feel when they do that "thing" is offense.

Now look in the mirror. Whether you're ready to accept it or not, there may be people in your life who potentially have festering wounds because you regularly offend them.

As you already know, we're complex humans with sensitivities that trigger offense. This means that the same grace we need when we're the offender is the same grace we may need to extend to others when they offend us. As you think about how you can navigate offense, here are a few actions to consider:

Be Aware

How might your words and actions impact others? How are their words impacting you? Ask the Holy Spirit to reveal if you've offended anyone or if what you're feeling is offense. Pray and ask for the strength to be the change or take actions to bring about change.

Ask and Seek Counsel

Offense triggers emotions. As our text for this reading reminds us, arguments create walls and barriers you can't break through. If you feel offended, ask the Holy Spirit to calm you so you don't say or do anything that hurts or offends. If needed, seek wise, Godly counsel, and be careful not to gossip.

Really Listen

Once you've calmed down, listen. Instead of focusing on your frustration, be curious. Ask questions, then listen. If you think you've offended someone, ask, "When XYZ happens, I notice [whatever you're experiencing]. Am I doing anything to offend you?" Or "When you do X, here's how it impacts me. Is there any way we can approach this differently?"

Every day, we connect and communicate, which means life will naturally create opportunities to offend or be offended. The beautiful thing is, with God's help and a few intentional steps, we can knock down those walls and heal those scabs.

Prayer

> Dear Heavenly Father,
>
> Every day, as I hurry about and engage in conversations, I'm sure there are family, friends, colleagues, and even strangers I've offended. There are also people, some very close to my heart, who offend me. God, make me more conscious of how I'm showing up and how others experience me. Please help me be calm, careful, and curious so my relationships can heal and be healthy. More than anything, please help me talk differently so when people see and hear me, they'll only see a reflection of You.
>
> Amen.

30

A VOICE THAT CHANGES THE ATMOSPHERE

HOW CAN YOU ADVOCATE FOR THOSE WHO HAVE NO VOICE?

"When I heard their complaints, I was very angry. After thinking it over, I spoke out against these nobles and officials..."
—Nehemiah 5:6–7 NLT

"**I'm done.**"

"I'm done with this place. They have nothing to offer me, nothing to teach me. How they speak and callously handle people is the real root of the problem. I'm done with it. Just done!" Those were the words she uttered in a moment of absolute frustration.

I paused and said to her, "You could quit. However, as believers, sometimes we're called to stay and bring something different to the spaces and places where we live and work."

One of my favorite leaders in the Bible is Nehemiah. Nehemiah was a cupbearer for King Artaxerxes of Susa. God led him to go back home to his people and rebuild the walls of Jerusalem, which had lay in ruins for over 140 years! Through a series of God-ordained events, he was given permission and resources from the king to return home and rebuild the wall. By the time we reach Chapter 5, the building project is going exceptionally well. The wall is half its full height.

Up to this point, even in the face of adversity, the people were willing to work on this project. One day, some of the men and their wives started to cry out in anguish. When Nehemiah asked what was going on, they exclaimed (in Leah's paraphrase), "We've been mortgaging our homes and even enslaving our children to our richer neighbors because we have no money, and we need grain to stay alive."

Nehemiah was furious and confronted the nobles and officials.

"How could you!" he exclaimed. "How could you charge interest and enslave your people! For years we've brought back our fellow Jews who were sold to Gentiles, and now you are enslaving your own people! What you're doing is not right," Nehemiah said. "The people need help. I and my brothers are lending the people money and grain."

Nehemiah then said to the nobles and officials, "Give them back their vineyards, olive groves, and the interest!"

The nobles agreed to return the people's belongings and children and swore an oath to keep their promise.

This conversation was a very bold move for Nehemiah. The walls were only halfway complete, and the nobles were quite powerful. The reality was he needed them to keep the project moving, so when the issue came up, he was in a pickle. He might have thought, *Do I say nothing or speak the truth and hope for the best?*

As we know, Nehemiah chose to speak, and in doing so, he saved the people and probably generations from possible oppression. On top of that, because he had the courage to speak up, the project did get back on track.

Every day, we encounter people and situations we don't agree with. Sometimes our greatest opportunity to bring about change might come by taking a risk to speak up for the people who need us most.

It's easy to get caught up in the politics of people and organizations. Feeling frustrated and fearful when we see inequities and exclusion around us is natural. However, when we put on our spiritual glasses, we'll see it's not the people, but the enemy wreaking havoc. Remember, your presence isn't an accident in these situations. God has placed you in that company, church, organization, or family for a specific purpose. The story of Nehemiah reminds us that when God is with us we can confidently speak because no person or situation can change His plan.

That day, as I wrapped up my conversation with the leader in the opening story, who is also a believer, we prayed. I asked God to give her the wisdom and strength to be the catalyst for change. For her impact to move beyond her technical skills and capabilities. We prayed that her actions and words would make her a vessel, not a victim, and her very presence would change the atmosphere. As we close out this pillar on talking differently, I pray this same prayer for you.

Prayer

Dear Father,

    There is so much injustice, pain, and frustration all around me. As a result, people are hurting, and situations sometimes spiral out of control. Some days I'm afraid to speak up or unsure if it's my place. In those moments, God, give me wisdom and courage. When I open my mouth, push the frustration or fear from my heart and help me to speak the truth in love. When I leave rooms and situations, help them not to see me but see You working through me.

    Amen.

Reflect & Renew

Conversations can be tough. Even when we're prepared and prayed up. As we wrap up this fourth pillar—Talk Different—take a few moments to reflect on the questions we've explored in our journey so far. Ask God to show you where He wants you to grow.

LISTEN DIFFERENT

1. Is it time to pause and listen for God's direction in your busy life?
2. How can you be more intentional about finding or creating space to pause?
3. Have you asked God to help you live out His plan for your life? If not, why?
4. What tribes do you have or need to build?

TRUST DIFFERENT

5. In what ways can you lean on God to help you fight and win your battles?
6. How might adopting the way God sees you impact your life?
7. What steps could you take to believe in your value even when you're not doing something big?
8. How might believing that God is in your tribe transform your confidence?

⑨ What voices do you need to quiet? What past victories can you remember?

⑩ In what ways has God used your past pain as preparation?

⑪ What steps do you need to take to stop comparing yourself to others?

⑫ How can you move forward using the strengths and gifts you have?

⑬ Where might God be calling you to influence change?

THINK DIFFERENT

⑭ How can you choose love and practice peace daily?

⑮ What thoughts or feelings about people might you need to let go?

⑯ What messiness in your tribe might you need to let in?

⑰ Knowing they'll never fully know you, what actions do you need to take?

⑱ Where are you experiencing values conflict? What does love look like even in conflict?

⑲ What offense might you need to let go?

⑳ What negative thoughts do you need to replace with action and boundaries?

㉑ Are the stories you've told yourself influencing how you love others?

㉒ What thoughts about situations and people can you give to God?

TALK DIFFERENT

㉓ In what relationships do you need to be more direct but not defensive?

㉔ What strategies could help you to pause before responding?

㉕ In what relationships might you need to stop avoiding conflict?

㉖ How can following Jesus' example transform your communication with others?

㉗ How is the tone of your voice impacting your communications?

㉘ Do you have a tribe that offers wise, Godly counsel? If not, who might you reach out to?

㉙ Do you experience offense in your relationships?

㉚ How can you advocate for those who have no voice?

Live DIFFERENT

PILLAR FIVE

Live Different

Welcome to the last pillar in our journey together—Live Different.

I don't know about you, but sometimes when I read a book, toward the end I start thinking about how I can practically implement the tools or principles in my life. In these last few pages, let's explore what being different could look like every day.

> It's the patterns of how we show up that tell people who and *whose* we really are.

31

OUT WITH THE OLD AND ON WITH THE NEW?

IN WHAT RELATIONSHIPS MIGHT YOU NEED TO EXTEND GRACE?

"...My servant Job will pray for you, and I will accept his prayer on your behalf. I will not treat you as you deserve..."
—Job 42:8 NLT

Every few months, someone will tell me they're glad they read my first book, *Assemble the Tribe*, because they need a new tribe. The reasons for moving on vary and might include:

- ∞ moving to a new location,
- ∞ taking a new job,
- ∞ wanting to learn a new skill, or
- ∞ even the death of a friend or relative.

But what happens when the tribe(s) you have can't help with—or distract you from—the life goals you have for yourself?

Let's talk. Would you answer "Yes" to any or all of these questions?

"Is it normal that life will sometimes cause relationships to change and people to grow apart?"

"Is it reasonable that you may not have the capacity (time, effort, or emotion) for old and new relationships?"

"In instances where the person no longer values what you value, or they live a lifestyle you no longer want to expose yourself to, would it be sensible to walk away?"

There are moments when it's absolutely time to walk away from relationships. However, when asked for advice, I often question if one needs to throw the relationship to the side or if it's simply time to love the person differently. As believers, the way we navigate these shifts matters a great deal.

As ambassadors for Christ, our number one priority is to share and live God's message of love. But how can we share that love if we push people and relationships to the side?

As I considered this puzzle for myself, I started to feel a little beat up as the Spirit asked me, "What if I treated you like you sometimes treat others? What if I decided that with all your flaws, you're too much work? What if I decided I'm done with you because you don't value what I value?"

The question becomes, how do we practically navigate this paradox? The delicate tightrope of God asking us to be open and love others when, in reality, we only have so much time, energy, and emotion to invest.

Here are two thoughts to consider:

Love Them Differently

When you're ready to move on, consider if you can invest in the relationship differently instead of ending it. Let's examine a scenario I often see play out. We'll use a fictional example of friends Heather and Alisha. What if, instead of pulling away, Alisha texted Heather occasionally or rang her up to check in? Imagine if Alisha told Heather she was grateful for the friendship. What if Alisha took the time to explain how the circumstances of her life were pulling her in different directions? What if she intentionally let Heather know any time she needed her, all she had to do was call? What if she reminded Heather their friendship mattered? When we care for people or invest in the relationship differently, we leave the door open to share God's love.

Remember God's Grace

Before you shut the door on a relationship, remember the grace God extends to you. The Book of Job shows a beautiful example of both divine and human grace.

Job's friends spent the entire book questioning Job's character and engaging in judgmental and unsupportive conversations that were likely very painful for Job. In Job Chapter 42:7-8 NLT, God tells Job's friends,

> *"...I am angry with you and your two friends, for you have not spoken accurately about me, as my servant Job has. So take seven bulls and seven rams and go to my servant Job and offer a burnt offering for yourselves. My servant Job will pray for you, and I will accept his prayer on your behalf. I will not treat you as you deserve, for you have not spoken accurately about me, as my servant Job has."*

The friends did as God commanded, Job prayed for them, and God accepted his prayer.

God made provision for Job's friends to be restored to Him even though He was angry and they didn't deserve it! Then there was Job, who despite their hurtful actions, was still willing to make the sacrifice on their behalf and call them friends. God may want to use your hands—like Job's—to extend grace to your connections, friends, or family in ways they don't deserve. The kindness and grace you share might pave the way for them to experience love and ultimately salvation. This is the potential power of our time, touch, and friendship.

There will be times when you need or want to walk away from a friendship. Before you pull the trigger and say "out with the old and on with the new," consider the opportunities your grace could create for someone else. If God believes you are worth it, maybe, just maybe, that person(s) in your tribe might be worth it, too.

Prayer

Dear Father,

   Relationships are complicated. I'm complicated. There were and will be times when I need to consider if I should show up and act differently in my relationship(s) or if it's time to walk away. Please help me be authentic and loving. Please help me not to be resentful, and show me how to create healthy boundaries. If it's time to walk away, allow me to find the right words so the door is always open to share Your love. Thank You for treating me in ways I don't deserve. I'm so thankful for Your grace.

   Amen.

32

A BLESSING WITH A BOUNDARY

WHERE CAN YOU IMPLEMENT BOUNDARIES WHILE STILL BEING A BLESSING?

"All you need to say is simply 'Yes' or 'No'; anything beyond this comes from the evil one."
—Matthew 5:37 NIV

"What are you doing?" I asked.

"Absolutely nothing!" she said.

"Nothing?" I replied.

"Yes, absolutely nothing! I told my family I've had enough, and I needed space! In fact, if they keep this behavior up, I will move out and check myself into a hotel!"

"What happened?" I asked.

Over the next nearly two hours, she shared with me in painful detail all the unkind words and actions she had tolerated, day after day, year after year, and now she'd finally reached her breaking point.

In Chapter 31, we explored how to move forward when relationships no longer serve us. In this reading, let's consider that perhaps the relationship isn't serving us because what we really need is to set a boundary.

A boundary is something that indicates or fixes a limit.[12] A limit is a real or imaginary point beyond which a person or thing cannot go. Sometimes we get a little twisted when we're trying to be like Christ. We try to be nice, quiet, giving, peacemaking, or accommodating when what is really needed is a boundary. I love the life of Christ because He demonstrated firsthand different types of healthy boundaries.

Wellness Boundaries

During His ministry, Jesus often left the group to find a quiet space early in the morning to pray. Despite the demands for His time, He set aside time for rest, solitude, and time with His various tribes. In doing so, Christ taught us to spend time with God and set time aside for self-care.

Request Boundaries

Jesus was teaching to a crowd one day when someone said, "... *Teacher, please tell my brother to divide our father's estate with me."* But Jesus refused to get involved and said, *"Friend, who made me a judge over you to decide such things as that?" (Luke 12:13-14 NLT)* My takeaway: there are times when it's okay to not get involved.

Values Boundaries

One day, Jesus entered the temple and saw people buying and selling animals for sacrifice. He knocked over the sellers' tables and told them, *"...The Scriptures declare, 'My Temple will be called a house of prayer,' but you have turned it into a den of thieves!" (Matthew 21:13 NLT)* The lesson is, sometimes you will need to stand up for what you believe.

Purpose Boundaries

When Peter tried to discourage Jesus from going to Jerusalem to suffer and die, Jesus recognized that Peter's words weren't in line with God's plan and said, *"...Get away from me, Satan! You are a dangerous trap to me. You are seeing things merely from a human point of view, not from God's." (Matthew 16:23 NLT)* This is a beautiful reminder that when God sends you on a mission, don't let anyone or anything take you off track.

We know Jesus had a heart for people and His tribe, but we see Him set boundaries repeatedly.

What can we take away from His examples?

Purpose Requires Boundaries

Boundaries protect our health and peace, which allow us to honor what God has asked us to do and who He has called us to be. When we try to be everything to everyone, we risk clouding God's voice and plans for our lives.

Boundaries Can Be Uncomfortable

Unhealthy requests or behaviors shouldn't be accepted or ignored. Get comfortable with being uncomfortable.

Boundaries Don't Release Us from Love

As people show us who they are and what they need, our response should be to love them. Love can take many forms, but we can also remember: Sometimes love needs to reside on the other side of a boundary. We can have limits to what we will and won't do.

This devotional reading's text is helpful when considering how best to approach setting boundaries. It says, *"All you need to say is simply 'Yes' or 'No.' Anything beyond this comes from the evil one."* (*Matthew 5:37 NIV*)

If there's something you know you shouldn't do or that will impact what God has asked you to do, your ideal response is to set a boundary. When we fail to set limits with people, frustration and resentment build and open the door for the enemy to destroy our relationships and disrupt our peace.

It doesn't matter what you have allowed in your relationships in the past. The good news is that you are not helpless. There's no relationship or situation that, with God's help, you cannot navigate in a whole new way. My prayer for you is that God will help you know when to say "No" and when to say "Yes" so you will be a blessing to others. And, when needed, a blessing from the other side of a boundary.

Prayer

Dear Heavenly Father,

So often I feel pulled to be loving and kind because I want to be more like You. But then it all gets twisted. I end up not saying what I mean, or I enable people in ways that hurt me and sometimes those around me. I ask for wisdom. Please help me to set healthy, respectful boundaries that protect my peace and honor You. Please give me discernment when others need to set boundaries with me. Boundaries are an area that comes up for me again and again because as I grow, my relationships evolve and change. Thank You in advance for helping me to be clear so I can always be a blessing with a boundary.

Amen.

33

WHEN FRIENDS BETRAY YOU

HOW CAN YOU LOVE EVEN IN THE FACE OF BETRAYAL?

"If you love those who love you, what credit is that to you? Even sinners love those who love them."
—Luke 6:32 NIV

Have you ever experienced the sting of betrayal?

Betrayal is when someone's action violates your confidence or trust.[13]

Many of us experience the most pain when someone betrays our hearts and does the unthinkable. Perhaps the unthinkable is they betray the things you shared with them in confidence. Or maybe instead of staying for the long haul, they do the unthinkable and simply walk away. Perhaps they lash out at you in hurtful and uncalled-for ways. Perhaps the unthinkable is conspiring with others against you.

In these moments, we are stunned, hurt, angry, confused, or disappointed, trying to make sense of what to do with the avalanche of emotions we didn't see coming. We're unprepared and ill-equipped to deal with what comes next.

The other day, I was coaching a friend about a situation where someone had said something hurtful to her. In isolation, it seemed like a moment of poor judgment, but as we talked it out, suddenly, the conversation became bigger. This was not just about this event. This was a pattern. As we talked it through, I could feel my friend wanting to pull back from the relationship. Now she knew it was just a matter of time before it happened again.

As we talked, I could sense her beginning to cut the mental and emotional ties. While she would've been within her rights to walk away, the Spirit nudged me to coach her differently.

We find the ultimate story of betrayal when we examine the friendship of Jesus and Judas Iscariot. What blows my mind about this story is that Jesus was fully God and fully man, able to understand the thoughts and hearts of men. However, as He carefully selected His tribe of twelve, those who would stand by His side and support Him in ministry, He chose Judas. When you and I select our tribes, we often can't know who someone is on a heart level. It's a pattern we discover over time. Yet here we have a situation where

Jesus knew Judas's heart and what would happen, and Jesus let him in anyway.

In my experience this isn't a normal reaction. For most of us, if we knew a friend was going to let us down, we'd run in the opposite direction as fast as possible. Who needs that kind of heartache and pain?

In my first book, *Assemble the Tribe*, I wrote a chapter on the benefits of relationship. In that chapter, I cited numerous studies that prove that poor-quality relationships impact our health and make us more susceptible to diseases like high blood pressure, cancers, and diabetes, which can send us to an early grave.

With so many reasons to walk away, Jesus still chose to keep Judas around. Why? Why should we ever willingly place ourselves in these types of relationships? At that moment, these words of Jesus came to mind:

> "If you love those who love you, what credit is that to you? Even sinners love those who love them. And if you do good to those who are good to you, what credit is that to you? Even sinners do that. And if you lend to those from whom you expect repayment, what credit is that to you? Even sinners lend to sinners, expecting to be repaid in full." (Luke 6:32–34 NIV)

"But God, that's such a tall order, " I said. "Not only are they likely to break my heart, but they're also bad for my health and happiness. I know You know this. Why would You want me to stay connected with people who are likely to hurt or let me down?"

"You need to be different when your friends betray you because, in the end, it's not about them. It's about you." Luke 6:35–36 NIV explains how:

> "But love your enemies, do good to them, and lend to them without expecting to get anything back. Then your reward will be great, and you will be children of the Most High because He is kind to the ungrateful and wicked. Be merciful, just as your Father is merciful.

Love, do good, AND lend—woah! Think about it. When we Live Different, God will reward and bless us in ways we can't imagine and call us His children. I believe Jesus chose Judas and allowed him to remain in His tribe to demonstrate that it's possible to be different, even when people aren't for us or don't love us how we expect them to.

Like we learned in the last chapter, we can be a blessing with a boundary. In situations of abuse, we might also need to walk away. Jesus never promised it would be comfortable or easy, but through His actions, He showed us it's possible to love, even when friendships betray us.

Prayer

Dear Heavenly Father,

I can think of many times when people disappointed me and let me down. People who were supposed to care for me and love me pushed a dagger into my heart. People who were supposed to be there walked away or failed to show up when I needed them most. God, take the pain away and show me how to love anyway. God, You know this isn't an easy task. Thank You in advance for doing what is impossible for me to do on my own.

    Amen.

34

ONE MOMENT AT A TIME

REFLECT ON A CHANCE ENCOUNTER THAT PROFOUNDLY INFLUENCED YOUR LIFE. WHAT DID IT CHANGE?

"Then, leaving her water jar, the woman went back to the town and said to the people, 'Come, see a man who told me everything I ever did. Could this be the Messiah?'"
—John 4:28–29 NIV

While writing this book, I spoke to a group of HR professionals about the importance of building one's tribe and being open. At the end of the speech, I shared a story about how a chance encounter with a man at a conference led to my first executive leadership position: Early on the morning of the conference, we struck up a conversation and I found out he had a big problem. We talked about the details over lunch. Early that afternoon, he had to return to the office to continue working through the issue. I gave him my card and said, "Call me if you ever need help." The next time he called, it was to ask me if I'd be interested in a role.

If you think about your life, I'm sure you can remember a few meaningful chance encounters. Here are two I discovered while writing this chapter:

When Albert Einstein was a young man in 1902, he had trouble finding work as a physicist. One day, he happened to meet a friend who worked at the Swiss Patent Office. This chance encounter led to a job offer that changed his life. Einstein worked there for several years while continuing to pursue his own scientific research. During this period, he developed his groundbreaking theories of relativity, which would revolutionize our understanding of space, time, and gravity.[14]

In the 1920s, Eleanor Roosevelt was a shy, reserved woman who had never been involved in politics. However, all that changed when she met Lorena Hickok, a journalist who covered Franklin D. Roosevelt's presidential campaign. The two women struck up a friendship that lasted for decades. Hickok encouraged Mrs. Roosevelt to become more politically active and use her position as the first lady to advocate for social justice issues.[15]

There are also many biblical stories of divine encounters: Jacob and God (Genesis 32:22–31), Moses and the burning bush (Exodus 3:1–15), and Ruth and Boaz (Ruth 2), to name a few. One powerful moment found in John 4:7–29 drew me in.

It's a sweltering day around noon, and even though you'd rather not, you know it's time to make the dusty trek to the well. With each step, the dry earth crumbles beneath your sandals. When you finally reach the well, you grasp the worn rope, lowering the heavy clay jar deep into the cool darkness below. Lost in your thoughts, you feel the familiar rope burn against your palms, when suddenly a voice cuts through the quiet:

"Ma'am, would you please give me a drink?"

You turn to see a man who is unmistakably a Jew sitting there. You glance around again, bewildered, unable to believe He's even talking to you. Memories of painful rejection flood your mind, filling you with a pain-tinged anger. You retort, "You're a Jew and I am a Samaritan. How can you even think of asking me for a drink?"

With gentle conviction, the man begins to speak. He talks of living water and that if you drink it, you will never thirst again. Intrigued by the gift He offers, and feeling the lingering burning in your hand, you ask Him for some of this living water. Perhaps then, you think, you could finally stop having to make the backbreaking trip to the well every day. Suddenly, the conversation takes an invasive turn.

"Go get your husband and come back to the well," He says.

He can't know, you think to yourself, so with an indignant voice, you say, "I have no husband."

With a quiet knowing, He responds, "That's true, you have no husband. But you have had five husbands, and the man you're with now is not your husband." Your hands begin to tremble as your heart beats faster and faster—*How can He know? Who is this man?*

As you look into His eyes, you expect to find judgment. Instead, you see only kindness. His gaze is piercing as if looking into the depths of your very soul. "You must be a prophet," you reply hesitantly. Not wanting to talk about your life of pain and rejection, you change the subject. You ask Him about the claims by Jews that Samaritans must worship in Jerusalem. As the man responds, you begin to feel something, something different. Your thoughts begin to wander as you listen to His words. *Could this be?* When He is finished, you say, "The Messiah is coming; when He comes, He will explain everything to us."

You look into His eyes, and all you can see is love and acceptance as He gently says, "I am the Messiah."

In the distance you see His friends returning. You gaze at the man one last time, and with a heart so full it feels like it might burst, you drop your water jugs and run back toward the town. Unable to contain the feeling of joy inside, you tell everyone, "Come see this man who told me everything I ever did. Could He be the Messiah?"

Moved by your passion, the people come out to hear Him in droves. He spends two days in your town and many listen to Him and believe. As the people learn more, and pass you on the streets, they say, *"…We no longer believe just because of what you said; now we have heard for ourselves, and we know that this man really is the Savior of the world."* (John 4:42 NIV)

I find it interesting and profound that the longest encounter between Jesus and any person in the Bible is with this unmarried, likely outcast, Samaritan woman. In a time and society when most would have simply passed her by, Jesus saw both her pain and her potential. Through their exchange, we witness truth, trust, and transformation—not only within her, but also through her.

Like the Samaritan woman, how many people around you are thirsty for love, kindness, and living water? Every day, we meet people from all walks of life and create moments: a harsh word, a kind word, an action, or inaction, can create ripples of change. I don't know about you, but for me sometimes this thought can be a little overwhelming; I mean, I was just short-tempered with a woman at the doctor's office this week!

The good news: God is a God of second chances. Like Jesus with the Samaritan woman, He sees beyond your faults and mistakes. God looks beyond your past into the potential of your future. All He is asking is for you to put your hand in His and allow Him to move in your life and the lives of everyone you encounter. You never know the impact your touch may have, one moment at a time.

Prayer

Dear Father,

Thank You for this powerful reminder of how impactful a single moment can be. Forgive me for all the times I was harsh or impatient with my family, my tribe, or even strangers. Every day I interact with those around me, help me to see them as You see them. Worthy, loved, and wanted, like the Samaritan woman at the well. God, help me to Live Different and show others You. I know for a fact I can't do this without You. I thank You in advance for working in me to help me become the hands You need me to be!

    Amen.

35

MOMENTS OF MARGIN

HOW MIGHT CREATING TIME MARGIN
INCREASE YOUR CAPACITY TO GIVE?

*"The generous will prosper; those who refresh
others will themselves be refreshed."*
—Proverbs 11:25 NLT

I was traveling from New York to California for the holidays. While I was standing in the security line at the airport, a woman stepped into the queue. It was hard to miss her because her baby was screaming at the top of his lungs. As I stood in line, churning through what seemed like hundreds of work emails on my cell phone, my thought was, *Why doesn't she just pick him up?*

I continued working for a minute or two, but the screams intensified. I put my phone in my pocket to investigate what was going on. When I looked closer, I saw why she couldn't pick the baby up. She had a purse, a baby carrier, a stroller base, and a small suitcase in her arms. I looked at her face and saw she was nearing her breaking point.

The agents ignored the baby and kept checking passports. I kept an eye on the mom, hoping they'd let her through, but no luck. Her eyes welled up a bit as she dropped a few things while bending down to pick up the baby, who was now screaming even louder.

At this point I walked over and picked up the suitcase and stroller base. I said to her, "Don't worry. I'll carry these two items for you."

Fifteen minutes later, the line continued to inch toward security at a snail's pace. By this time, the baby was inconsolable.

Behind us, a gentleman spoke up and said to the mom, "I know exactly how you feel. I have a two-year-old and a three-year-old. I recently traveled with both of them to Singapore. I promise it'll be okay."

He then asked her about her flight departure time. She said, "At this point, I don't think I'm going to make it. My flight leaves in twenty minutes."

He said, "Oh no, these people will let you through. You will not miss your flight today!"

Like a knight in shining armor, he stormed through the line, baby seat overhead as he pushed her to the front. I had to follow because, at this point, I was the bag carrier! Finally, at security screening, we rushed to unpack her stuff. I was deep in her bag, digging through diapers and pulling out laptops while simultaneously unpacking my carry-on so we could get through as quickly as possible. Now it's fifteen minutes until departure!

We got through security in record time. I realized her gate was quite a distance away. Ten minutes to departure. At this stage, she thought I would leave her, so she started to break down a little, and I said to her, "Don't worry, my gate is on the way. I'll stay with you until you get on the plane."

At that moment, we heard an announcement: "Flight 104 to Miami, final boarding call; please make your way to the gate." Five minutes to departure.

Picture this: two grown women huffing and puffing, barreling through the airport, bags and screaming baby in tow! We had no choice but to run across the terminal, down an escalator, across again, up another escalator. We were a sight!

When we reached the top of the second escalator, she started to run again but was exhausted by the baby's weight.

I said to her, "Don't worry, I'll run to the gate for you!"

I took off running to Gate 35, thinking to myself, "Why does it have to be so far away?"

I finally made it to the gate. The attendants tried to whisk me on board. I was so out of breath I could barely talk. Gasping, I said, "No, it's not me. It's a lady with her baby. They're coming now."

Within ninety seconds the lady and baby arrived. When she realized she would make the flight, she started to cry. She asked my name, hugged me, and with tears streaming down her face said, "Thank you so much!"

Mission accomplished!

As I watched her make her way down the jetway, my exhaustion melted away. I felt at peace. My plan for the afternoon was to use all my spare time in the security line and at my gate for emails and calls, but God had another plan. However, I'd almost missed it because of my busyness.

Life is hectic. With our long to-do lists, we have zero "margin" (breaks you intentionally create in your day). When you think about it, doesn't that feel like a creative trap of the enemy? To keep you so busy and overwhelmed you don't have time to be God's hands to those around you?

When we are generous with our time and resources, not only will God favor us, but He will also bless others through us. In Chapter 34, we were reminded that life happens and changes in moments. As we close this reading, consider how you can create more moments of margin in your life to be a walking, talking, practical blessing every day.

Prayer

Dear Father,

Thank You for this reminder to slow down. Most days, there's so much to do I'm blind to the needs of those around me, even in my own home. Help me stop surviving the busyness and thrive in moments of margin so I can be Your hands and share Your love.

Amen.

36

A PRAYING TRIBE

WHO WOULD BE VALUABLE ADDITIONS TO YOUR PRAYER TRIBE? IS IT TIME TO REACH OUT?

"But while Peter was in prison, the church prayed very earnestly for him."
—Acts 12:5 NLT

Do you have a person or tribe that's your go-to when life gets tough?

Many years ago, I was navigating a complicated situation with a work colleague. I called a good friend to vent and get it off my chest. For over an hour, she listened to me share the details and examples of how this person made my work experience a nightmare.

After she had listened for a while longer, she said, "Leah, I'm so sorry you're experiencing this situation. Now, let's pray."

Let me set the stage a bit better: This was a big deal. I was upset, angry, hurt, and frustrated. I was in my feelings, and I just wanted to be heard. When she asked me to pause in the middle of my meltdown to pray for this person who was making my life a living hell, my first thought was, *No, I'm not praying for this person. I'm the one who is suffering; you need to pray for me!*

I remember what happened next as if it were yesterday. My friend said, "Well, if you're not going to pray, I will."

Before I could open my mouth to say another word, she launched into prayer for my colleague. She prayed for their family and their success. She prayed for their health and their heart. She prayed her prayer would travel into every nook and cranny of the individual's life. The prayer was so powerful that when she stopped talking, all I could do was say, "Amen."

I no longer had the energy or desire to vent. My best next step was simply to let the prayer do its work.

We find another example of powerful prayer in the Book of Acts. In Acts Chapter 12, Herod is on the warpath against believers. He has arrested some of the believers and had James, John's brother, put to death. Now, he has arrested Peter. Peter is such a formidable leader of the early church that Herod instructs him to be guarded by four squads of four soldiers each. That's sixteen men to guard one man in chains!

In Acts 12:5 NLT, the Bible says: *"But while Peter was in prison, the church prayed very earnestly for him."*

The church continued to pray intensely, and the night before Peter's trial, an angel came to him and said, *"...'Quick! Get up!' And the chains fell off his wrists. Then the angel told him, 'Get dressed and put on your sandals.' And he did. 'Now put on your coat and follow me,' the angel ordered."* (Acts 12:7-8 NLT)

Peter's escape was so incredible even Peter thought he was dreaming. When Peter eventually found his tribe, what were they doing? Before, during, and after his escape, that's right, they were praying.

When life throws its inevitable challenges our way, sometimes we look for our friends so we can get things off our chest. Sometimes that's the right move. The Bible even says, *"Where there no counsel is, people fall; but in the multitude of counselors there is safety."* (Proverbs 11:14 NKJV)

However, what if, like Peter's tribe, we also chose to earnestly pray?

James 5:16 KJV gives us clear instructions on what to do to see God move. It says, *"...the effectual fervent prayer of a righteous man availeth much."*

In the original Hebrew, the word effectual is *energeó,* which means to bring something from one point to the next.[16]

Take that in. Your prayers and the prayers of your tribe have the power to shift outcomes from one thing to another.

As we wrap up this devotional reading, you might be wondering what happened with my colleague. Shortly after my prayer with my friend, I decided my best next step was to have a conversation with my colleague. In the end, it worked out, and my colleague's life was blessed in a life-altering way.

My challenge to you is this: the next time you or someone from your tribe is navigating a challenging situation, pause to pray. God is there. He's always waiting, willing, and wanting to be a part of your tribe.

Prayer

> Dear Heavenly Father,
>
> I can accurately pinpoint the last time I should have invited You into a conversation. Thank You for this reminder to include You in every area of my life. God, surround me with women and men who know how to pray. Help me wherever and whenever possible to be the catalyst that boldly brings prayer into the lives of others. Thank You for always being a part of my tribe.
>
> Amen.

37

LOVING DIFFERENT WHILE LIVING DIFFERENT

WHAT STRATEGIES CAN YOU USE TO LOVE YOURSELF WHILE LOVING OTHERS?

"'Martha, Martha,' the Lord answered, 'you are worried and upset about many things, but few things are needed—or indeed only one. Mary has chosen what is better, and it will not be taken away from her.'"
—Luke 10:41–42 NIV

Jesus and His disciples were traveling to Jerusalem when Jesus decided to make a pit stop at Martha's house. Martha loved Jesus and welcomed Him and His disciples into her home. She understood Jesus. Martha understood all the places He had been, the people who followed Him from place to place wanting to hear Him, to be touched or healed by Him. Martha understood He had a mission that drove Him to the brink of exhaustion and sometimes He put the needs of the people above His own.

So when Jesus stopped by her house, Martha decided His experience had to be different. She would pamper Him, give Him a comfortable place to rest, and prepare the best meal He had had in weeks. Never mind that Martha would have preferred some notice. He was here. With a burst of adrenaline, she switched into preparation mode. The fire was stoked, the pots came down, and the fish was marinated while the vegetables and the bread were prepared. Martha intuitively knew the steps to follow with each dish she tackled. There was so much to do!

When Martha looked up to assign Mary two more tasks, she was surprised to discover Mary was nowhere to be found.

Martha mused, "Where is she? Does she not know that Jesus is here? Doesn't she know Jesus is tired and hungry and needs to be fed?"

A little exasperated and singularly focused on ensuring Jesus had everything He deserved, Martha set out to find Mary. Martha searched out the back with the cows; maybe Mary was getting some milk, but no Mary. Martha looked at the side of the house; maybe Mary was in the herb garden picking some fresh thyme for the soup, but when she turned the corner, still no Mary. Martha looked all over, not once considering Mary might be with the men. However, having exhausted every other logical space in the house, Martha looked into the meeting room. And there she was.

Quietly sitting by the side of Jesus was Mary, engrossed in His every word, having completely forgotten the soup she was supposed to be prepping. Martha's insides began to boil as she marched into the room and said, "...Lord, doesn't it seem unfair to you that my sister sits here while I do all the work? Tell her to come and help me."

"'Martha, Martha,' the Lord answered, 'you are worried and upset about many things, but few things are needed—or indeed only one. Mary has chosen what is better, and it will not be taken away from her.'" (Luke 10:41-42 NIV)

As a consummate organizer and arranger, I can imagine the emotional roller coaster Martha must have experienced in that moment. Wanting to do and give Jesus her very best, only to be left to do it all by herself, and now Jesus was telling her perhaps there was a better way. Perhaps there was, but who would finish preparing all the food?

Have you ever felt like Martha? You're doing your best to love someone with all your heart only to have them tell you they need something different? Perhaps you sent a text, but they really wanted a call. You showed up to the meeting on time every time, but what they wanted was for you to tell them they're doing a great job. You called and said, "If you ever need anything, I'm here for you," but they wanted you to show up on their doorstep and sit with them while they cried.

This story and line of thought open the door for us to examine how we love. In just a few verses before this story, in Luke 10:27, we're admonished to love our neighbors as ourselves. Meaning our default when loving others is to ask ourselves, "If this was me, how would I want to be loved?"

With the best of intentions, we try to love as if the other person were in our shoes, only to find it gets all confusing. In our efforts to love them as we love ourselves, we often find our efforts rejected, misunderstood, or underappreciated.

Jesus understood in the years that followed, so many of us would read Luke 10:27 and then do our best to love others as we love ourselves. I believe He intentionally stopped by Martha's house to give us some advice when our love meets resistance.

He knew Martha. He knew even though she loved planning, she loved Him and would welcome Him into her home. After feeding the five thousand, He was exhausted. He knew His time was coming to an end, and as He carried the weight of His mission, He needed an oasis, a place to stop and simply be taken care of. He would find this at Martha's house. He knew she would love Him as she loved herself.

However, in that simple, gentle exchange starting with "Martha, Martha," Jesus demonstrates we must not see loving others like we love ourselves as the only way we love. Instead, it is the key that unlocks the door to loving others the way they need to be loved.

Martha was wired to love by doing, but Jesus gently reminded her that sometimes love isn't about doing.

When you reflect on how you love, you might find you're on the right track or you might find you need to make some changes. No matter where you are, this story, so strategically placed on the pages of Luke, reminds us there are different ways to love and we'll always be a work in progress. Today and every day in the future is an opportunity to Love Different while we Live Different and simply try again.

Prayer

Dear Father,

    I believe You when You say the keys to unlock the door to the kingdom require me to love others. All these years, I have done my best to love others as I love myself. Sometimes that has worked, and sometimes I have experienced resistance and rejection, which has hurt me to the bone. God, please help me to Be Different. To love with a pure heart even when it hurts. As I try my best, please show me how to love the way others need it most. Help me Love Different in my home, at my job, in my church, and in my community. Thank You for loving me enough to stop by Martha's house to show me another way.

    Amen.

38

LOVE ANYWAY

WHAT WOULD IT LOOK LIKE TO LOVE WHEN PEOPLE DISAPPOINT YOU?

"Then he returned to the disciples and found them asleep. He said to Peter, 'Couldn't you watch with me even one hour?'"
—Matthew 26:40 NLT

Have you ever found yourself surrounded by your tribe but still feeling alone? Perhaps you were struggling with an illness, processing the loss of a family member, or simply overwhelmed by life. In these moments, you wanted your tribe to be there, but no one called or stopped by to check in. You felt let down and wondered if they cared.

You aren't alone. In fact, Jesus knows exactly how you feel because He lived it while He was on Earth.

Jesus knew His mission was about to be fulfilled. He stole away to the Garden of Gethsemane in deep emotional agony. He knew the only way to find strength and power was to spend time with His Father. In His grief and distress, He asked his inner circle (Peter, James, and John) to sit, keep watch, and pray. Instead of praying, they let Him down by falling asleep and leaving Him to fend for Himself, not once, but twice! You can read the full story in Matthew 26:36–46.

What do we do when we find ourselves in these painful moments when we ask, *Where are my people? Where are the church folks who profess to love me? Where are my friends when I need them the most?* Through His words and actions, Jesus modeled how to Live Different. Let's explore together:

Go to the Source

The scene in the Garden of Gethsemane provides clear instructions on what to do when we're at our lowest point. Jesus knew with every fiber of His being that God was the source of His strength (Isaiah 41:10), His rock (Psalms 18:2), and His ever-present help in trouble (Psalms 46:1). In His darkest moments, He spent time alone with His Father in prayer. In our most difficult moments, our first response should be to talk to our Heavenly Father.

Take Off Your Mask

Has someone asked you how you are, and, knowing full well you're not okay, you say, "I'm okay"? When Jesus found Peter, James, and John sleeping, He didn't pretend it didn't matter. He was direct. "Could you not stay awake even for an hour?" Jesus asked for help, and in doing so, He demonstrated that sometimes we need to tell people what we need. Remember, there's a zero percent chance of support if people don't know we need it.

Forgive

At no point in the following few chapters leading up to His death do we see Jesus have another exchange with Peter, James, and John. At no point did He pull them up on the carpet for failing to be there when He needed them most. Instead, in the final verses of Jesus' story in Matthew 28:16–20, Peter, James, and John are commissioned to go into the world and make disciples with the promise that Jesus will be with them until the end of the age.

Jesus knew the hearts of His tribe. He knew that Peter, James, and John loved Him. Jesus also knew they were imperfect, capable of falling asleep and denying Him. Instead of reacting to their failure, Jesus simply considered the pattern of how they loved Him over the course of His ministry, and He forgave them.

Focus on Your Assignment

It's reasonable to assume there are other times throughout Jesus' ministry where He wanted His disciples and friends to be there for Him. The truth is, they were never going to be there because Jesus was on assignment. Their support, or lack of support and even betrayal, was part of God's plan to save the world. Similarly, sometimes we're hurt because our tribe isn't there in the way we want. However, their absence doesn't mean they don't love us. Perhaps they're not meant to be there because their presence or actions might interfere with our assignment.

I know relationships are complicated. Sometimes it's hard to know if the hurt we experience is intentional or unintentional. But everything that happens in our lives is designed to give us the tools to help someone else or shape the only thing that matters: our character.

Character isn't an accident; it's the result of choices and actions intentionally practiced. This is what it truly means to Live Different: to stare all the facts in the face and say, "I can choose how I respond. I can choose to be vulnerable or I can choose to create a boundary. I can choose to let it go or I can choose to talk it out. And no matter what, I can always choose to love anyway."

Prayer

> Dear Heavenly Father,
>
> Sometimes, I'm so wounded by those I expect to be there for me. In these moments, help me come to You first, for You are the source of everything I need. At times, help me to be honest and vulnerable so others can see and understand my needs. Please help me remember all my interactions and relationships are part of my assignment. Give me a heart to love unconditionally. I know when I can love like that, it will be You working in me, and that is what I want more than anything.
>
> Amen.

39

WITH ALL YOUR HEART

WHAT IS GOD CALLING YOU TO SHARE
WITH ALL YOUR HEART?

"Whatever you do, work at it with all your heart, as working for the Lord, not for human masters, since you know that you will receive an inheritance from the Lord as a reward. It is the Lord Christ you are serving."
—Colossians 3:23–24 NIV

Ignaz Semmelweis was a Hungarian physician born in 1818.[17] He received his doctor's degree from the University of Vienna in 1844. His first job was as an assistant at an obstetric clinic in Vienna. Upon starting his career, he soon noticed most women gave birth at home, but some women were hospitalized because of poverty or complications. These women faced significantly higher mortality, sometimes as high as 30 percent. The common view at the time was that the problem, also known as puerperal or childbed fever, was caused by overcrowding, poor ventilation, the onset of lactation, or polluted vapors.

Dr. Semmelweis was so disturbed by what was happening that he decided to figure it out. Even though his chief didn't support him, because he believed the disease was unpreventable, Dr. Semmelweis discovered the mortality rates dropped significantly when the medical students washed their hands with chlorinated water before examining patients. In fact, after implementing the new procedures in his division, he saw the mortality rate drop from 18.27 percent to 1.27 percent. Even in the face of such extraordinary results, his medical colleagues were hostile and critical of his work. In fact, the editor of a medical journal in Vienna wrote, "It's time to stop the nonsense about the chlorine hand wash."

Dr. Semmelweis wanted his work to be accepted to save lives, and he worked at it with all his heart. However, in 1861, after his work was largely rejected, he became increasingly angry and frustrated. From that year on, his health began to deteriorate, which later resulted in his being committed to an asylum where he died at the age of forty-seven. Tragically but ironically, he died from an infection caused when the guards beat him during his admission.

Despite all that, Dr. Semmelweis is recognized as a pioneer of antiseptic procedures and is known as the "father of infection control." His work shows how societal and cultural factors limit or impede progress. However, perseverance, passion, and dedication can impact lives for generations, sometimes in ways we will never know.

I would guess you've probably had a Dr. Semmelweis moment. If I were sitting with you right now, I'm sure you could describe your pain when the depth of your love, commitment, passion, and sacrifice is misunderstood or overlooked.

In the Bible, the stories of women are often overlooked or untold. Like Dr. Semmelweis, the role of women was often seen as irrelevant or unimportant. The reason why is debated. In ancient times, societies were patriarchal, and men held most of the positions of authority. It's also possible that women were excluded from the Bible due to cultural bias or religious beliefs. Women were also less educated, and their stories were not recorded or preserved to the same extent as men's.

One thing I love about the life of Christ is that women are included. From the call of His mother, and even Elizabeth (mother of John the Baptist) before her, we find their stories throughout His ministry—the woman caught in adultery, the woman with the issue of blood, and the woman at the well. Mary and Martha. The widow of Nain. Joanna, Susanna, and the other women who followed Jesus and provided financial support to His ministry. The women at the cross, and even Mary seeing Him first after His resurrection at the tomb—at every turn, women are part of His ministry.

Though the details of their lives are often sparse, the stories of these women are retold again and again. Their lives unlock our imaginations, inspire change, and fill us with hope. These women were many times unseen, but they were exactly where God wanted and needed them, and they loved Him with all their hearts.

Please, never forget that what you have to give makes a difference, even when you're overlooked or misunderstood. Like Dr. Semmelweis and the many women, when you give to others, your contributions, work, and stories can impact lives and reach places you may never go.

So, write the book, start the ministry, love on that ornery person you see every week at church, speak softly to your spouse or unruly child, help the stranger, check on a senior, be kind to that colleague who refuses to help you. You never know what God will do when you love and live with all your heart.

Prayer

> Dear Heavenly Father,
> I want to live for You. But sometimes giving hurts. It hurts to make a difference only to be overlooked or misunderstood. Father, I know it shouldn't matter, but sometimes it's painful. God, show me how to give. Please show me if I'm getting in the way of being Your hands. I'm so grateful for this reminder that when no one sees me, You see me. Please help me to remember living differently for You with all my heart will always be enough.
> Amen.

40

SALT

HOW DOES YOUR LIFE IMPACT THOSE AROUND YOU? IS GOD CALLING YOU TO MORE?

"You are the salt of the earth. But what good is salt if it has lost its flavor? Can you make it salty again? It will be thrown out and trampled underfoot as worthless."
—Matthew 5:13 NLT

Most women in their mid-to-late forties and older know maintaining a healthy weight is like crossing the ocean in a kayak. Over the years, I've tried all kinds of plans and programs. I've seen doctors and tried supplements. Still, my ideal state of health and weight has eluded me. In recent years, as the more intense symptoms of perimenopause have begun to set in, I've started to appreciate the intricate complexities of how our bodies are designed even more. The hot flashes impact sleep, blood pressure, and mood, to name a few!

Many of us struggle to escape this problematic, vicious cycle. Raise your hand if you're with me!

As we age, our metabolism slows. Without altering what and how much we eat, the food we ate five years ago that helped us lose weight might cause us to gain weight today. To combat this cycle, I've had to accept that I must eat very differently whether I like it or not.

One day, I decided to make black bean soup from scratch. My goal was to reduce the amount of sodium in it. I soaked the beans for two days, cut the vegetables, seasoned the soup with herbs, and dumped everything into the slow cooker.

The soup was cooked to perfection in just under six hours. The beans and vegetables were soft, and I pureed half of the mixture, which produced a beautifully rich, textured black bean soup. Not bad for a first try. The smell was amazing. I leaned over to give it a taste, but I almost spat it back out because it had no flavor.

I didn't want to add salt, so I added more seasoning: paprika, cumin, Mrs. Dash, onion powder, and red pepper flakes. I stopped to taste it again; it was better, but it needed more. I found a garlic-and-black-pepper mix and generously added it to the mixture. All of a sudden, the flavors of the soup opened up. It was as if I were eating a completely different dish. The soup I wanted to spit out a few moments before went down like comfort food.

The change in flavor profile was so dramatic I returned to the bottle to look at the magical ingredients. What was in the blend?

And there it was, the first ingredient on the list: SALT!

Our journey to live differently is a lot like my health journey and that soup pot. All our lives, we've struggled to navigate complicated relationships—with ourselves and others—often stuck in patterns that feel impossible to break. But what if we could be like salt?

In the Sermon on the Mount (Matthew 5), Jesus spoke about salt and what kingdom living looks like. He knew the Jewish people, who valued sharing meals, would understand the metaphor. Salt doesn't have to try—when added, it changes everything.

As we close out our time together, always remember: You need people, and they need you. The truth is, relationships will never be easy, but you—with all your gifts, talents, and strengths—are part of His plan. You were placed on Earth to touch lives and change everything they understand about love and God. As you leave this moment, please never forget: God hears you, loves you, and needs you. Today and every day, He invites you to be His hands on earth—just be salt.

Prayer

> Dear Heavenly Father,
>
> For so long, I've wanted connection. I've wanted to find my community, my tribe. I've wanted to experience relationships that comfort and bring me joy. God, I believe this is possible. However, I accept it won't happen as I

thought it would. Not everyone is going to respond. Not everyone is going to love me. But my relationships and every encounter will shape me and change me, and I'll change situations and shift atmospheres. Help me always know and believe that when I stay open and share Your love, You will meet my relationship needs.

I give my relationship journey to You. Help me to be salt. Use me. Be the architect of how, when, and where I experience the love You know I need on this Earth. I thank You because You will always be more creative and intentional than I ever could be.

Amen!

Reflect & Renew

It's one thing to know we need to Be Different. However, it takes work to consciously and intentionally change the way we love and interact with people. As we wrap up this fifth pillar—Live Different—take a few moments to reflect on the questions we have explored in our journey. Ask God to show you where He wants you to grow.

LISTEN DIFFERENT

1. Is it time to pause and listen for God's direction in your busy life?
2. How can you be more intentional about finding or creating space to pause?
3. Have you asked God to help you live out His plan for your life? If not, why?
4. What tribes do you have or need to build?

TRUST DIFFERENT

5. In what ways can you lean on God to help you fight and win your battles?
6. How might adopting the way God sees you impact your life?
7. What steps could you take to believe in your value even when you're not doing something big?

⑧ How might believing that God is in your tribe transform your confidence?

⑨ What voices do you need to quiet? What past victories can you remember?

⑩ In what ways has God used your past pain as preparation?

⑪ What steps do you need to take to stop comparing yourself to others?

⑫ How can you move forward using the strengths and gifts you have?

⑬ Where might God be calling you to influence change?

THINK DIFFERENT

⑭ How can you choose love and practice peace daily?

⑮ What thoughts or feelings about people might you need to let go?

⑯ What messiness in your tribe might you need to let in?

⑰ Knowing they'll never fully know you, what actions do you need to take?

⑱ Where are you experiencing values conflict? What does love look like even in conflict?

⑲ What offense might you need to let go?

⑳ What negative thoughts do you need to replace with action and boundaries?

㉑ Are the stories you've told yourself influencing how you love others?

㉒ What thoughts about situations and people can you give to God?

TALK DIFFERENT

㉓ In what relationships do you need to be more direct but not defensive?

㉔ What strategies could help you to pause before responding?

㉕ In what relationships might you need to stop avoiding conflict?

㉖ How can following Jesus' example transform your communication with others?

㉗ How is the tone of your voice impacting your communications?

㉘ Do you have a tribe that offers wise, Godly counsel? If not, who might you reach out to?

㉙ Do you experience offense in your relationships?

㉚ How can you advocate for those who have no voice?

LIVE DIFFERENT

㉛ In what relationships might you need to extend grace?

㉜ Where can you implement boundaries while still being a blessing?

㉝ How can you love even in the face of betrayal?

㉞ Reflect on a chance encounter that profoundly influenced your life. What did it change?

㉟ How might creating time margin increase your capacity to give?

㊱ Who would be valuable additions to your prayer tribe? Is it time to reach out?

㊲ What strategies can you use to love yourself while loving others?

㊳ What would it look like to love when people disappoint you?

㊴ What is God calling you to share with all your heart?

㊵ How does your life impact those around you? Is God calling you to more?

FINAL THOUGHTS:
The Chameleon Effect

While writing this book, I had just left a professional tribe. As a person who values and accelerates with community, this change left a big hole in my life. In my quiet moments, I asked God to help me find a new tribe to fill the void, a community to help me grow. A few days later, I received an email invitation, and at the eleventh hour. I mean at 11:59 p.m. with a midnight deadline. I signed up for a writing class! This was my new tribe.

During one session, the instructor said we wouldn't cover the planned content for the day. Instead, she felt led to ask us to think about our purpose. While on a break, someone popped on camera and asked the group, "How's everyone doing?"

As we went around the room, someone said, "The attacks are so heavy for me right now." At that moment, I felt compelled to speak.

You see, it just so happened that week, I had been studying this text: *"He gives power to the weak, and to those who have no might, He increases strength."* (Isaiah 40:29 NKJV)

I shared with the group that often we might feel weighed down by the day-to-day realities of life and the pain we see all over the world.

During my devotion earlier that week, I was curious: What was this "power" the text offered?

I looked up the word in the original Hebrew language. The word "power" is translated from *koach*, pronounced ko-ah.[18] Usually, the definitions of Hebrew words are clear to me. However, on this day, I was confused. You see, *koach* means a small reptile. Sitting there, I thought, "What on earth does a small reptile have to do with power?"

As I read the words *ability*, *able*, *might*, *power*, and *strength*, things started to make more sense. However, right in the middle, there it was again: *chameleon*. I asked again, "God, what does this have to do with your power?"

Then the Spirit said, "The power I want to give you is the power to become different, the power to change, adapt, and survive in any situation." In the room with my new virtual tribe, I shared this thought.

A few minutes later, the instructor came back on camera from break. She asked me to repeat what I said to the group. I shared again. Then the God-ordained tribe moment began. The instructor and the group iterated with the idea that a chameleon is different and becomes different. As we batted that idea around for a few minutes, a new level of clarity began to emerge.

While we were talking, I googled *what makes a chameleon so unique?*

As we close out this book, I invite you to accept the call to "Be Different," which was so cleverly clarified and confirmed through this unscheduled, unexpected exchange about a lizard and why it's so unique. You see…

Chameleons Can See in Two Different Directions

God is inviting you to experience life and relationships differently—starting by listening to His voice. Where you see rejection, perhaps there's grace instead. Where you see walls, maybe there's a path through. Where you see an ending, maybe there's a new beginning. When we listen to His voice, He opens our eyes to see our relationships in new ways—ways that may seem unnatural to those around us.

Chameleons Can Regulate Their Temperature

As you commit to trusting different and thinking different, God will begin to regulate your heart and thought life. As God transforms you from the inside out, you'll be more confident in who He created you to be. Your thought life and expectations of others will change as well. What once felt hot and uncomfortable and would push you over the edge will roll off your back. Instead of boiling, unrestrained anger or crushing fear, you'll have the mindset to tackle life's challenges with clarity, authenticity, courage, and love.

Chameleons Can Change Color to Signal Their Intentions to Others

When you accept the call to Talk Different and Live Different, you'll say things you never meant to say. You'll do things you never meant to do and go to places you never meant to go. God will transform everything about how you show up in the world. You'll know with 100 percent certainty that as you Live Different, you'll signal to everyone who you are: God's hands on earth.

Until Christ returns, I can guarantee with 100 percent certainty that relationships will never be easy. Sin is complicated. People are complicated. Inevitably, relationships are complicated. However, when you choose to Listen Different, Trust Different, Think Different, Talk Different, and Live Different, through the power of the Holy Spirit, He will reconstruct your heart, reconfigure your nature, and grant you the power to be His hands on earth and change the world.

> *For His divine power has bestowed on us [absolutely] everything necessary for [a dynamic spiritual] life and godliness, through true and personal knowledge of Him who called us by His own glory and excellence. For by these He has bestowed on us His precious and magnificent promises [of inexpressible value], so that by them you may escape from the immoral freedom that is in the world because of disreputable desire, and become sharers of the divine nature. For this very reason, applying your diligence [to the divine promises, make every effort] in [exercising] your faith to, develop moral excellence, and in moral excellence, knowledge (insight, understanding), and in your knowledge, self-control, and in your self-control, steadfastness, and in your steadfastness, godliness, and in your godliness, brotherly affection, and in your brotherly affection, [develop Christian]* **love [that is, learn to unselfishly seek the best for others and to do things for their benefit]***. (2 Peter 1:3–7 AMP)*
>
> *For you have been called to **live in freedom**, my brothers and sisters. But don't use your freedom to satisfy your sinful nature. Instead, **use your freedom to serve one another in love**. For the whole law can be summed up in this one command: "Love your neighbor as yourself." But*

if you are always biting and devouring one another, watch out! Beware of destroying one another. (Galatians 5:13–15 NLT)

No one has seen God at any time. **But if we love** *one another [with unselfish concern],* **God abides in us**, *and His love [the love that is His essence abides in us and] is completed and perfected in us… And this commandment we have from Him, that the one who loves God should also [unselfishly] love his brother and seek the best for him." (1 John 4:12, 21 AMP)*

BE DIFFERENT

ACKNOWLEDGMENTS

First and foremost, I want to thank God for allowing me to be the author of this book. Usually, when we read a book or watch a movie, we're excited about the hero or heroine. We delight in watching their backstory and discovering their strengths or superpowers. We revel in their transformation journey and cheer as they conquer the seemingly impossible. However, as I have written, read, and reread this book in the editing process, I've never had that feeling. If anything, I've felt guilty that I still need to work on one pillar or the other. Through this process, God has repeatedly reminded me that, like you, I will always be a work in progress. As inadequate as we might often feel, God loves us anyway, differently.

To my husband, Terry, and to Tristan and Taylor, thank you. You see things others can't. You see and live my battle and journey to Be Different every day. More than anyone, you have a front-row seat to my inadequacies, but you still love me. Thank you. To my mom and dad, siblings, nieces, and nephews, I love you and appreciate you more than you'll ever know.

Thank you to my wise beta readers—Mom, Michelle, Ann, Phelecia, Simona, Michelle P., and the many friends who have read pieces of this book: You have helped me make it better. To my editor, the amazing and very patient Arlene Gale, thank you for combing through this book and helping me to make it better. To the publishing team at Scribe, it's been a pleasure to do this again!

To my tribes that have traveled life's journey with me for years, even those of you that I only see every now and again, but when we do, it's real, thank you! I need you more than you'll ever know.

To my local church family, conferences, and organizations that have allowed me to share my expertise and experiences with your leaders, teams, and people, thank you for the opportunity. My time with you has incubated thoughts that made it to the pages of this book. You have allowed me to see with clear eyes how God can use us to be His hands.

Last but not least, thank you to you, my reader! You chose to spend time with me, giving me one of the things in life you can never get back: your time. I pray that your time in these pages has given you some practical tools and touched your heart. If it has, I would love to hear from you. Email me at hello@leahjmdean.com or message me on any of my social platforms.

As you close the pages of this book, more than anything, I want you to know God loves you and you'll always be a work in progress, and that's okay. The journey to Listen Different, Trust Different, Think Different, Talk Different, and Live Different will always be there. The good news is God designed it this way because all He wants is you. In the pages of this book, He's given you a bold blueprint, You have the tools and steps; now it's time to take action and be His hands on earth.

Never lose hope, and never give up. Every day is an opportunity to begin, fail, and simply start again.

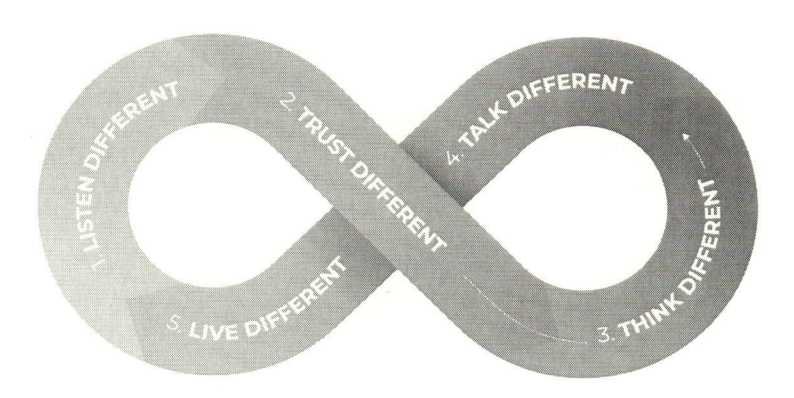

1. LISTEN DIFFERENT
2. TRUST DIFFERENT
3. THINK DIFFERENT
4. TALK DIFFERENT
5. LIVE DIFFERENT

BE DIFFERENT

A SPECIAL
Invitation

Now that you've reached the end of *Be Different*, I'm thrilled to invite you to take the next step by joining the *Be Different* Bonus Portal. This special space is packed with tools, assessments, and so much more! Everything in the portal is designed to inspire and support you on your journey to be God's hands on earth.

To dive in and explore these exclusive resources created just for you, visit www.leahjmdean.com/bedifferenttribe. I can't wait for you to experience it all!

See you inside!

Leah xo

ABOUT THE
Author

LEAH JM DEAN is the CEO of Conduit International Ltd., a professional and personal development solutions company dedicated to helping organizations and women work smarter, live well, and foster meaningful connections. With over two decades of experience, Leah has shaped leading HR strategies and served as a trusted coach and advisor to thousands of leaders, employees, and women across the globe. She has worked across diverse industries, including insurance, reinsurance, education, nonprofit, faith-based, financial services, food and beverage, and business consulting.

A self-proclaimed recovering workaholic, Leah is passionate about inspiring women to find strategies to enjoy their work, invest in their well-being, and make a lasting impact on the lives of those they touch. When she is not working, Leah enjoys reading, writing, walking in nature, and spending quality time with family and friends. She lives in Bermuda with her husband. Terrance. and two children.

Leah would love to connect with you wherever you call home. You can find her at:

- ∞ Instagram: www.instagram.com/leahjmdean/
- ∞ LinkedIn: www.linkedin.com/in/leahjmdean/
- ∞ Facebook: www.facebook.com/leahjmdean

Visit www.leahjmdean.com to learn more, subscribe to our monthly newsletter, and enjoy free resources.

BRINGING *BE DIFFERENT* To Life

Are you ready to bring *Be Different* to your women's group or organization? In this interactive experience, Leah shares the simple framework for the woman who wants to discover how God can transform our relationships through our daily, sometimes momentary, choices.

Using real-life examples, stories, research, and activities, Leah's group experience will help every woman in your audience discover that all this time, she's been waiting for kingdom-building relationships to come to her, not realizing that they're going to come through her.

To inquire about a possible speaking engagement, please contact Leah via her website at www.leahjmdean.com/contact or email her team at hello@leahjmdean.com.

A SPECIAL *Request*

A good book can change a life, and it can create ripple effects when shared with others.

As you finish *Be Different*, take a moment to reflect. What was your biggest takeaway? How did this book help and inspire you? I hope it has equipped and encouraged you in many ways. If so, I'd be deeply grateful if you'd take a moment to help others in your tribe, in your world of influence, to discover *Be Different*. And your tribe will be grateful to you, too.

- ∞ Share your experience by posting a review at your favorite online bookstore.
- ∞ Snap a picture and post it on social media, telling others how the book touched your heart.
- ∞ Send a note to a friend who would love it—or better yet, surprise them with a copy!

Your thoughts and reflections could be the spark that inspires someone else's journey of transformation. Together, let's share the message of *Be Different* and make an even greater impact in the world!

MORE BOOKS BY
Leah JM Dean

Your tribe could just be the thing that changes everything.

In *Assemble the Tribe*, Leah Dean unveils a simple yet powerful formula for finding, building, and transforming the way readers connect and experience the power of sisterhood. With authenticity, she shares personal stories and real-life applications. You'll also find inspiring stories of women whose lives have been transformed by the power of support. Dive into these pages and discover how to unleash your unique value; build deep, meaningful relationships; and find the support you need to grow. Perfect for any woman seeking more connection, more empowerment, and a more fulfilling life.

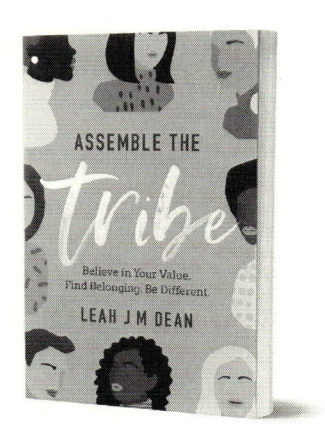

Visit www.assemblethetribe.com to download the first chapter for free or listen to an audiobook sample. *Assemble the Tribe* is available on Amazon.com and wherever books and e-books are sold *(now in audiobook format)*.

BIBLE Translations

In this book, I reference several Bible translations, including the NIV, AMP, ESV, NLT, KJV, and NKJV, to offer a well-rounded understanding of the scriptures. All direct citations have been marked in italics. All citations are sourced from Bible Gateway, ensuring consistency and clarity in the presentation of these texts.

Amplified Bible. (2015). The Lockman Foundation. https://www.biblegateway.com/versions/Amplified-Bible-AMP/ (Original work published 1964).

The Holy Bible: English Standard Version. (2001). Crossway. https://www.biblegateway.com/versions/English-Standard-Version-ESV-Bible/ (Original work published 2001).

Holy Bible: King James Version. (2020). Thomas Nelson. https://www.biblegateway.com/versions/King-James-Version-KJV-Bible/ (Original work published 1611).

Holy Bible: New International Version. (2011). Zondervan. https://www.biblegateway.com/versions/New-International-Version-NIV-Bible/ (Original work published 1978).

Holy Bible: New King James Version. (1982). Thomas Nelson. https://www.biblegateway.com/versions/New-King-James-Version-NKJV-Bible/ (Original work published 1982).

Holy Bible: New Living Translation. (2015). Tyndale House Publishers. https://www.biblegateway.com/versions/New-Living-Translation-NLT-Bible/ (Original work published 1996).

ENDNOTES

1 *Merriam-Webster Dictionary*, "significance," accessed August 11, 2024, https://www.merriam-webster.com/dictionary/significance.

2 *The Redeem Team*, directed by Jon Weinbach (distributed by Netflix, 2022).

3 "1515. eirēnē," Strong's, Greek, Bible Hub, accessed August 9, 2024, https://biblehub.com/greek/1515.htm.

4 Margot Lee Shetterly, "Dorothy Vaughan," NASA, last modified August 5, 2024, https://www.nasa.gov/people/dorothy-vaughan/.

5 "2344. thésauros," Strong's, Greek, Bible Hub, accessed August 9, 2024, https://biblehub.com/greek/2344.htm.

6 "3341. metanoia," Strong's, Greek, Bible Hub, accessed August 9, 2024, https://biblehub.com/greek/3341.htm.

7 "3326. meta," Strong's, Greek, Bible Hub, accessed August 9, 2024, https://biblehub.com/greek/3326.htm; and "3539. noéō," Strong's, Greek, Bible Hub, accessed August 9, 2024, https://biblehub.com/greek/3539.htm.

8 Leah J. M. Dean, *Assemble the Tribe: Believe in Your Value. Find Belonging. Be Different* (Houndstooth, 2020).

9 Andrew Newberg and Mark Robert Waldman, *Words Can Change Your Brain: 12 Conversation Strategies to Build Trust, Resolve Conflict, and Increase Intimacy* (Hudson Street Press, 2012).

10 "Loose Lips Might Sink Ships," Nabb Research Center Online Exhibits, Salisbury University, accessed August 9, 2024, https://libapps.salisbury.edu/nabb-online/exhibits/show/propaganda/slogans/loose-lips-might-sink-ships.

11 *Merriam-Webster Dictionary*, "offense," accessed August 9, 2024, https://www.merriam-webster.com/dictionary/offense.

12 *Merriam-Webster Dictionary*, "boundary," accessed August 9, 2024, https://www.merriam-webster.com/dictionary/boundary.

13 *Merriam-Webster Dictionary*, "betrayal," accessed August 9, 2024, https://www.merriam-webster.com/dictionary/betrayal.

14 Biography.Com Editors and Tyler Piccotti, "Albert Einstein," Biography, last modified July 20, 2023, https://www.biography.com/scientist/albert-einstein.

15 Biography.Com Editors, "Eleanor Roosevelt," Biography, last modified March 6, 2024, https://www.biography.com/political-figure/eleanor-roosevelt.

16 "1754. energeó," Strong's, Greek, Bible Hub, accessed August 9, 2024, https://biblehub.com/greek/1754.htm.

17 *Encyclopædia Britannica*, "Ignaz Semmelweis," by Imre Zoltánlast, last modified October 19, 2024, https://www.britannica.com/biography/Ignaz-Semmelweis.

18 "3581. koach," Strong's, Hebrew, Bible Hub, accessed August 9, 2024, https://biblehub.com/hebrew/3581.htm.

Made in United States
North Haven, CT
07 March 2025